9.95

Western riding

D0583292

DATE DUE

WESTERN RIDING

WESTERN RIDING

Your Self-Teaching Guide

DON ZOLL

Photographs by Louise Whitney

David McKay Company, Inc.
New York

For R.A.
with gratitude

Library of Congress Cataloging in Publication Data

Zoll, Don.
Western riding.

Bibliography: p.
Includes index.
1. Western riding.   I. Title.
SF309.3.Z64   798'.23   79-12999
ISBN 0-679-51452-X

1 2 3 4 5 6 7 8 9 10

MANUFACTURED IN THE UNITED STATES OF AMERICA

ACKNOWLEDGMENTS

My thanks to my friend Bill Mowery, one of the nation's premier cutting horse trainers, for placing the facilities of his ranch near Carefree, Arizona, at my disposal for the shooting of instructional photographs. My thanks, too, to Jim Marshall, proprietor of the H-M Horse Farm of Kirkland, Illinois. Jim has been a major factor in the encouragement of cutting in the Midwest.

I also wish to express my appreciation to John Hoyt, Jr., who played the role of the "student" in these photographs. John is in fact an extremely experienced rider for his years. He is the son of the well-known trainer, John Hoyt, Sr.

I would also like to thank the American Quarter Horse Association for its permission to reproduce parts of its "blue book" for this volume.

The author would like to acknowledge the kindness of the principal photographer for this book, Miss Louise Whitney. Louise is also the talented editor of *The Arizona Horseman*. With equal gratitude, my thanks to Judith Yuenger, the accomplished equestrian photographer from Westchester, Illinois.

Many people have extended numerous kindnesses to me during the preparation of this book. Not the least among these has been my wife, Madge, who stoically endured the process of my attempt to distill over thirty years of teaching horsemanship into the reasonably brief treatment of this book.

D.Z.

CONTENTS

Introduction:
What About
Riding Self-Taught?

Riding a horse is an applied art—and it is an "art." It cannot, of course, be entirely learned from a book. Reading is no substitute for hours of pounding around in the saddle. But hours in the saddle without some notion of what you're trying to accomplish are equally frustrating. Try learning to play a guitar without some kind of an instructional manual.

Books deal in theory, and theory is very useful when you get around to the business of taking on an "applied art." The trouble with theory, frankly, is that it only deals with general cases. Take horse training as an example. A lot of people think there are mysterious tricks to it—known only by a small guild of professionals. The fact is that virtually everything known about training the horse is contained in books. The reason you can't become a horse trainer only by long visits to the public library is that all books on training horses talk about some general, abstract, hypothetical horse—and the one that you set out to train is a real live *individual* horse, complete with all the maddening variations of personality and aptitude that horses come with. At this point, experience must augment theory; the problems presented by "real-world" horses have to be faced and solved.

1

So part of learning to ride involves coping with individual horses. Each one is different and each one will teach you something, even after years of experience, if you have the flexibility of mind to appreciate the subtle differences. Books cannot replace this intangible adaptability.

But where would you be without the theory, the principles, the methods? The general rules provide a basis for dealing with the complex of exceptions. General rules are adapted, then, to specific cases, in other words, and so it is with learning to ride. Horsemanship involves getting the vital experience that dealing with assorted horses provides, but the education of the horseman begins with theory and, for that, books provide a handy means.

Let's be practical, though. Books have their limitations. I can't quite see the eager student, mounted on his horse, one hand holding the reins, the other the "instructional manual," like a patient parent assembling his kid's new bike. Reading this book, or any book, is a *preliminary* step toward "putting the foot in the stirrup."

Why not take lessons? After having spent most of my adult life teaching horsemanship, I can hardly disapprove of the lesson approach, the direct student-instructor method. But utilizing this approach may be easier said than done. There is a very real shortage of qualified teachers, particularly those who specialize in the "stock seat." Not everyone lives conveniently close to a first-class riding school—and really top-notch western riding schools are not all that common. Many people who yearn to ride "western" simply don't have access to formal instruction. These people must go it alone—hopefully with the help of this book.

Of course, human beings have been learning to ride for centuries without the aid of books, although treatises on horse-mastership are very old. The earliest one that has been preserved was written by Xenophon, a Greek who lived at the time of Socrates.[1] Certainly few, if any, westerners in the last century learned to ride from a book or any other way, for that matter, except by just doing it, perhaps with a friendly suggestion here

[1] Xenophon (c.430–c.355 B.C.) was a rather extraordinary personality who managed to be both a mercenary soldier and a historian, besides his apparent interest in the management of the horse. While his treatise is mostly of historical interest (he lived long before the invention of the stirrup), certain familiar items appear, such as the use of the snaffle bit.

2

and there. That's a tough method. It was literally true, by the way, that some young drovers actually learned to ride a horse simply by getting aboard and trailing cattle; read the memoirs of Frank Harris for illustration.

Beyond the fact that it doesn't make much sense to do things the hard way, the fact of the matter is that "natural" (or primitive) horsemen had their limitations. A certain amount of skill can be acquired by repeatedly doing something the wrong way. My technique at the typewriter is a good example. I can rattle the machine pretty well (without benefit of the approved methods), but I could type a great deal better if I'd taken the time to learn how to do it correctly in the first place. Also the primitive horseman (the Cossack, the Indian, the old cowboy) was restricted in terms of versatility. Theory permits one to adapt, to intelligently vary techniques to suit circumstances.

I knew a woman once who was about as well informed about *dressage* as anyone I have ever met.[2] Her knowledge was encyclopedic. However, she couldn't ride a horse down to get the mail, as they say, although she fancied herself as an accomplished horsewoman. In this instance, theoretical understanding didn't translate into performance, and many an illiterate cowhand can ride rings around more learned enthusiasts. But it is not an either-or situation. "Wet saddle blankets made good horses" is a very sensible old western maxim; it could be adapted to read, "Wet saddle blankets are necessary if you want to become a skilled horseman." But it is not necessary or intelligent to try to reinvent the wheel, so to speak. Experience *accompanied* by theory (which is, after all just accumulated and recorded experience reflected on) not only makes learning an art easier and quicker, it also makes it far more efficient.

The main problem in attempting self-teaching, even with the best theoretical aids at hand, is the problem of criticism and correction. In the ring, the student can pause and ask his instructor, "How am I doing?" and get an answer. This being a

---

[2] *Dressage* is a French term meaning "training." It has come to mean the formal training of the horse by the use of exacting techniques of balance and suppleness introduced by a high refinement of the rider's aids. Correspondingly, it has also come to refer to a rather specialized form of equestrian competition or spectacle stressing those qualities, especially in the so-called *haute école* or "high school" phases of dressage.

book and not a correspondence course, what I have tried to do is to anticipate many of these questions, presume the little difficulties that usually arise, and give you some "road signs" by which to judge your progress, as well as to offer help in overcoming the more common types of difficulties. I also have to make some perhaps artificial assumptions. In preparing this book, I felt I had to assume that most who would use it would be adults, or at least not small children, and not of an age where physical limitations would be a serious factor. While I imagined that my readers were primarily interested in pleasure riding, I also took it for granted that they would ultimately be intrigued by either taking part in various western equestrian games (like cutting or roping) or in show-ring competition, as well as pleasure and trail riding. I have taught children as young as four, by the way, and I once made a pretty fair cowboy out of a sixty-two-year-old man who previously had never swung up on a horse, but these extremes of age call for some rather sharply modified techniques that I will not go into in this volume. I also figured that those who will use this book as a guide will have access to a suitable horse and gear and can find a ring or corral to work in.

This matter of appropriate equipment is worth discussion. Any serious progress will depend on what you have to work with. And that, first-off, includes the horse you intend to learn to ride. Contrary to what you might think, horses useful for instructional purposes are hard to come by. Over the years, I've conducted a more or less constant search for good school horses, and finding them is no cinch. They are hard to find because a beginner's horse must be gentle and tolerant, but a great deal more than a phlegmatic "dude" horse. A satisfactory horse to learn on is prompt and responsive to the hand and leg aids, as well as consistently quiet and honest. A horse that is at once free-going and extremely steady for beginners—including timid beginners— is a "find," but without a horse of that description it is next to impossible to make much progress as a riding student. If you own such an animal, count yourself fortunate. But if you have to acquire one, you may have a problem on your hands. This is not a treatise on "how to buy a horse," but I can make a few quick recommendations. Perhaps the best general source of instructional horses is the privately owned "pleasure" horse that hasn't quite style enough to make the show ring. Sometimes, too, honest

4

ranch horses are suitable if they've been gently handled. It's sensible not to start with a young horse; find one that is settled and past its post-adolescent flings, certainly a horse over six years of age. Find a horse that suits you, size-wise. Generally, the size range is from 14.2–15.2 hands. A beginner's horse must have a decent "rein"; it need not be really quick, but it must rein well enough to perform "school figures" like a figure eight. While I'd urge you to pass up, as a rule of thumb, ex-livery and "school" horses, don't worry too much about the animal's age and looks if it meets the other qualifications.

The correct choice of a saddle is crucial. You may be picking one out for the first time, and western saddles come in a bewildering collection of sizes, styles, and shapes. Some types of saddles, otherwise excellent, are for very specialized uses and are far from being ideal for beginners. In general, the best saddles to learn to ride on are either standard roping saddles or "cutting" (general purpose) saddles. The most important feature in either of these types is a reasonably flat seat, at least one in which the deepest part of the dip is approximately midway between the pommel and the cantle, or between the front and rear. Avoid like the plague those so-called "equitation" saddles, now being merchandised, that have sloping seats that shift the rider away from the horse's center of gravity. These strange saddles also have vast amounts of foam padding behind the "swells" or pommel fork of the saddle that make it next to impossible to stay in balance with the horse. The beginner's saddle should have a relatively low cantle (not over three inches), but probably a little more cantle than is common in extreme, slick-front ropers. A moderate swell fork, a feature of cutting and general purpose saddles, is not objectionable, but exaggerated, over-wide swells with sharp leg undercuts are not only unnecessary but constitute a downright handicap for elementary instruction. All unusual features can be easily dispensed with, like over-sized roping stirrups, tapaderos, dally horns, and so on. Two-inch stirrups, Visalia or Bell type, are recommended. In short, your first saddle should be simple and orthodox. The beginner doesn't yet know what "game" he wants to play eventually, so his gear must be not too specialized. Later, you can indulge your newly acquired preferences for more extreme styles, if you like.

Many people choose saddles that are too long in the tree.

5

The roping-type saddle. This is an excellent saddle for instructional use. Note that the seat is not too deep. The oxbow-type stirrups are optional.

The cutting-type saddle. Also an excellent saddle for the beginner. It is low in the front and has a relatively shallow, flat seat. There is somewhat more swell and cantle than is usual in a roping saddle.

Saddles, incidentally, are measured from the top of the cantle to the back of the swell. Most women do very well in fourteen-inch saddles and men in fifteen-inch ones. Most standard, production-line saddles come in these sizes. There are many individual cases, of course, where larger or smaller saddles are called for. Don't try to ride in a saddle that is too long in the tree. What is "too long"? Once seated in balance, the rider's trunk should not move back and forth on the saddle; he is not wedged between the pommel and cantle, but being in the middle of the saddle he does not slip back against the cantle. The horse's center of gravity is located in the *withers* (the juncture of the neck bone and the spinal column). You can discover it as a small hump just ahead of the pommel of the saddle if you're feeling for it while aboard. A saddle that is too long for you will shift your weight inadvertently toward the cantle and away from where the action is, too far from the center of gravity.

Horses suitable for beginners ought not to need unusual bits or restraining devices. A "cowboy" snaffle or a low port curb are the appropriate bits, used in a simple headstall. Use split reins. *Romals* (California-style reins braided into a quirt at the terminal end) or connected roping reins are not recommended while learning. Try to use heavy reins that are at least six, and preferably seven, feet long in order to get a proper "feel." As a rule, tie-downs or martingales are unnecessary for beginners' horses.

Then there is the matter of your personal equipment. It is not necessary for western riding to wear an elaborate "habit." Blue jeans (not necessarily always blue) are almost universal. There are, though, certain pieces of gear that are almost indispensable. You *can* ride in shoes of various sorts (but don't try to ride in soft, rubber-soled ones). However, a pair of boots is a virtual necessity, and you might as well start out with a proper pair—not "engineer's" or "work" boots—a conventional pair of western boots. Boots are not a place to economize. The best you can afford are not only the most comfortable, but are also the most economical in the long run. Get them fitted by someone who knows his business—and be patient during the "break-in" period. After awhile, they'll feel like carpet slippers, but for a week or so they'll hurt your feet. The thing to do is to bite the bullet and

7

wear them as much as you can, not just when you ride, and they'll begin to shape around your feet.

Wear a hat. It won't improve your riding, but it is both traditional and functional. Gloves are a matter of choice or taste, but they'll save you some blisters and some people (including myself) prefer the feel that gloves give.

Later on, you will likely want to add spurs to your gear. There is a lot of misunderstanding about spurs. Spurs are nothing more than a metal extension of your heels. They allow you to effect the leg aids without actually using the heel, pulling it out of its proper position. In this sense, spurs are an integral part of a horseman's equipment. They are not used primarily for punishment or to make the horse run faster! But they should *not* be worn until the rider's heel position is totally stabilized, insuring that he does not hit the horse with the spur by accident. The style of western spurs is traditional, with long shanks and rowels of various patterns. This style makes them appear rather awesome. In fact, you could use a pair of blunt, English-type spurs almost as efficiently, but western spurs are no more severe than conventional forms of the English spur. Like saddles, western spurs come in a variety of specialized patterns, some used for roping, cutting, and so on. The "green" rider is best off with a short-shanked, small-roweled, "all-purpose" model.

I cannot resist the temptation to suggest that chaps be an early investment, granted that to have a pair made will more or less decimate a hundred dollars. After becoming used to riding in chaps, you get the feeling of being naked without them. They increase the feel, the purchase, the rider gets on the barrel of the horse, being like a soft glove into which the leg fits. Their comfort—except, perhaps, in one hundred-plus temperatures—is very substantial. The most common style—universally used now in the show ring—is the fringed "shotgun" type, often with California-style tapering legs that fall, when mounted, well below the stirrup. The other type, the "batwing," is still favored by cutting horse riders and a large proportion of working hands. They come in a wide variety of leathers, including, I regret to say, a rainbow of colors. Perhaps there is a place in the show ring for pale blue or lavender chaps, but I am unconvinced. When it comes to gear, from saddles and bridles to chaps and shirts, my best advice is to lean toward the somber, rather than the flashy.

The urge to ride a horse is very ancient. The origins of mounted horsemanship, by the way, are murky and still in scholarly dispute. Horses apparently pulled chariots long before someone got the notion to swing aboard and sit on their backs. Whoever did originate riding, it's been a technique that has not only changed human history, but has fascinated people long after riding ceased to be a practical necessity. The horse population of the United States doubled from 1960 to 1970 and it is expected to double again by 1980, the overwhelming majority of these horses being used for recreation and the vast percentage of them being riding horses.

I always figured that somebody ought to do a really scientific study of the psychological relationship between man and the horse. I don't think it's a simple matter, this pull the horse has on the human psyche. I'd even go so far as to say that there are people who *need* horses, have a "compulsion" about them, I suppose a psychologist would term it. It's almost an addiction—but not a corrupting one; I seem to remember Winston Churchill saying something to the effect that young men have "gone wrong" by wagering on horses, but never from riding them.

Whatever is the reason, more people than ever are eager to learn to ride and to keep horses. But a part of that romance of man (and woman) and horse involves what I call the "riding into the sunset syndrome": the illusion, doubtless influenced by movies and television, that all a person has to do is to swing his leg over a horse and then ride, happily and carelessly, into the sunset. Why else do people simply rent horses and suppose that they can ride off without trouble, people who would not jump into twenty feet of water if they couldn't swim or drive a car without knowing how it operated? People are not prepared, often, to respond to the physical and mental disciplines, the sheer hard work, that horsemanship requires. This problem comes up largely because the horse is an animal, and fewer and fewer people grow up these days in close contact with animals, particularly a large animal such as the horse. I have found in my experience that in teaching, one of the important objectives is simply to introduce students to the horse as an animal. That is not always easy to do within the nominal operation of a riding school where students get only limited experience with horses beyond the mounted work in the ring. The aim of instruction must be

9

horsemastership, if that is not too ponderous a term. Riding, alone, is not enough; it must be combined with a growing knowledge of the horse, and that is gained by dealing with the horse in a wide variety of situations, from taking care of the animal to training and using it. This is one of the advantages of horse ownership, if the owner really undertakes the serious care or supervision of his horse. In learning to ride, it may be a handicap to own a horse and therefore be restricted, more or less, to only one horse, in contrast to the riding-school student who may ride a number of horses. On the other hand, the horse owner—including a large number of the readers of this book—has the favorable opportunity of relating to his horse in a wide variety of ways, of coming to understand what "horsemastership" really means.

It is often forgotten, particularly by a conscientious riding student, that the aim of riding is not how well the rider "sits" or even how effective are his aids, but how excellently the horse performs. The art is aimed at the performance of the horse. This means that riding and training are inseparable activities. A real horseman "trains" a horse every time he sits on it, even if he is not actually engaged in a training session. The horse ridden by a master horseman improves from the experience, even if the time involved is slight and the improvement only minute. That is the harsh standard against which even the beginner must begin to measure himself. The horse one uses for elementary instruction does seem like a sort of passive instrument, a "training aid," but there is a transition in the education of the rider where the emphasis, as we shall see, shifts from preoccupation with what the rider is doing to attention to what the horse is doing. It is at that point when the "game" gets truly interesting.

Of course, most people take up riding for fun. That's a pretty good reason for doing anything. Sure, it's fun. But the fun increases with skill. Everyone has his own definition of fun, but mine is working a really sharp stock horse. I've had students become downright mesmerized the first time they had the opportunity to actually work live cattle from the back of a horse; it was almost as though they were suffering from the "rapture of the deep" that divers are supposed to encounter when they go too deep. Even elementary instruction can be fun if it's approached with both a capacity to work hard and to retain a sense of humor.

Teaching riding and writing this book have been sources of satisfaction, because they involved sharing the fun that horsemanship can provide. But it is rather high-level fun, I think. This is why this book makes a serious effort to put western horsemanship in a solid theoretical frame, to treat it as the art that it genuinely is. The book is written in the belief that even the "Sunday rider" really wants to acquire solid skills and to attain performance levels that will permit him to gain the fullest satisfaction from horsemastership, to be a part of that grand tradition that is centuries old.

1

The Western Horse and Horsemanship

Western horsemanship may appear to have a relatively brief history. After all, "western riding" is identified with the American West, the "cowboy" era of the last century. It could be seen as some regional style that grew up in the range cattle industry. Perhaps, too, it is even an anachronism these days as the need for the skills of the cowman are quickly passing, at least outside the rodeo arena.

These ideas seem to be supported by the fact that "how-to-do-it" books on eastern or "English" horsemanship far outnumber those on western equitation. Perhaps one explanation for this imbalance is the fact that many people suppose that western horsemanship is primitive, less sophisticated, less artistic than the English style, and that it lacks both a long history and a theoretical base.

Despite these prejudices, western horsemanship not only grows increasingly popular in North America but also it is being widely exported abroad for both work and recreational purposes. This persistent popularity grows, I firmly believe, from something more solid than nostalgia or the common, if erroneous, idea that western riding is "easier" to master or that it is "safer" (presumably because the saddle horn serves as a safety handle). The fact of the matter is that the western system of horsemanship enjoys a very old historical ancestry and demands skills and knowledge quite as sophisticated and artistic as the approach to horsemanship that originated in northern Europe in the seventeenth century.

It may be possible to argue that the roots of western horsemanship derive from the very origins of the art—the horsemastership of peoples of the Eurasian Steppe that introduced most of the essential aspects of horsemanship, including the stirrup and divided trousers. But it is difficult to talk very precisely about ancient methods, except for the fact that mounted warfare appears to be an Oriental development, meaning that the birthplace of horsemanship took place amid the vastnesses of the Near East where warriors went into battle on light, tough, desert-bred horses, depending for success on mobility and quickness.

But to be more historically exact, the origins of modern-day western horsemanship and, indeed, the western horse itself are Spanish. The development of the Spanish system of horsemastership deserves a brief account.

For about seven centuries, the Spanish peninsula was partially inhabited by Moorish invaders from North Africa. The struggle that went on along the line "where the olive grows" was between these Moslem Africans and the Visigothic kingdoms of northern Spain. These were cavalry wars, fought between the heavy, mounted, feudal chivalry of the Christian states and the light horse of the Moors. The Moorish horsemen were the direct descendants of all Oriental cavalrymen; they were swift, hard-hitting skirmishers, mounted on the blooded desert horses we today can identify as the Arabian and the Barb. They scorned body armor, used light saddles and short stirrups, and favored the lance and the scimitar (the ancestor of the saber). In contrast, the Visigothic chivalry, consistent with their origins, were knights, the armored horsemen of Europe, slow-moving and employing the heavier horses necessary to bear the weight of full armor. The feudal knight was virtually wedged into his high-backed and -fronted saddle, his stirrups hardly raised enough to bend the leg.

In the progress of these wars—usually more in the nature of border raids than sustained campaigns—the Spanish gentry were not slow to appreciate the advantages of the Moorish style of horsemanship, as they tended to be attracted to most things Moorish, with the exception of the religion. They readily adapted many features of their enemies' techniques and equipment. As a matter of fact, they also began to breed horses, using the essentially Barb stock of the invaders. The result, incidentally, was the Spanish horse, the war horse highly prized, world-wide, for centuries, the remaining example today being the pure-bred Andalusian. Without wholly abandoning the traditions of feudal men-at-arms, the Spanish developed their own particular highly mobile cavalry called the *genetes,* adopting the Moorish style of riding with shortened stirrups, lighter saddles, and weapons. This Spanish light horse was widely admired well through the sixteenth century.

The appearance of the *genetes* encouraged the Spanish aristocracy to create a both elegant and functional style of horsemanship that placed a primary emphasis on quickness of maneuver, handiness, and the calm obedience of the horse, all virtues made possible by the breeding of their splendid chargers. The medieval saddle had given way to a radically modified military type that, while preserving the raised pommels and cantles, was greatly reduced in weight and incorporated quilting on the seat and a much simplified stirrup. This style of horsemanship and the equipment that accompanied it was the method employed by the *conquistadores* in the New World.

The long conflict between Christians and Moors in Spain has been described as a border war, a continuous state of raiding comparable to the Indian-fighting days on our own frontier. There is another similarity. A very considerable livestock industry had grown up on the peninsula. The adversaries in this war of raid and counterraid were often otherwise occupied in cattle herding. The Spanish-Moorish style of horsemastership was equally adaptable to war and livestock husbandry.

Spanish colonialization in the New World, especially in North America, featured the establishment of vast ranching enterprises for which the Spanish mode of riding and their evolving equipment was excellently suited. But the demands of large-scale cattle work and the availability of huge herds of domestically bred horses (bred from the original Spanish stock) encouraged new skills and techniques. With remarkable speed, the Spanish gentlemen ranchers (the *charros)* and their drovers (the *vaqueros)*

14

shaped traditional Spanish horsemanship to their immediate needs, creating the training methods that produced the world's first specialized "cow horse." Many of the institutions one associates with the range cattle industry are Spanish, including the use of the *reata* (the braided rawhide lariat) and branding, among others. The Spanish introduced some remarkable training methods that have rarely if ever been excelled, using the bosal hackamore and a variety of what we now term "California-style" bits, the Spade and the Half-Breed. The Spanish saddle which evolved in Mexico and California was the progenitor of all "stock" saddles. Like the original saddle of the *conquistadores,* this saddle was constructed on a split tree, but it now featured a huge horn on which to dally the *reata,* tapadero-clad stirrups, and a center-fire cinch.

The original inhabitants, the Indians, and the Anglos who were beginning to filter into the trans-Mississippi West immediately grasped the practicality of the Spanish methods and equipment. When an American cattle industry was established on the Great Plains, the Spanish techniques were appropriated, with some changes and embellishments. The early Texans (or Texicans, as they preferred to be called at this time) did not like the exposed tree of the traditional *Charro* saddle and so they covered it with a permanent skirting. They preferred "grass" ropes to rawhide ones, and they liked split reins as against the *romal.* But from head to foot, hat to spurs, with chaps thrown in, everything they used had a Spanish origin. They rode on pseudo-Spanish saddles (although they developed the double-rig, as the Texans liked to rope "hard and fast" rather than to dally) and rode like their Latin predecessors, perhaps with a bit more rustic nonchalance.

But the advent of the great cattle trails north to the Kansas railheads after the Civil War sharply altered the style of western horsemanship. The long days of constant work in the saddle placed a natural emphasis on comfort. The Texas saddle of this period featured extremely high cantles, and stirrups were worn very long so as not to cramp the knee. The horses of this era, while admirable in some respects, were hardly the spirited chargers of the *charro,* carefully schooled to the lightest direction of the rein. What had emerged was the "fork seat," the basic mode of western riding until well into the twentieth century. Using short-treed saddles, the drovers and cattlemen of the period sat against their cantles, their bodies literally "forked" into the saddles by the use of long stirrups that held the leg virtually straight.

Even the army rode this way. Since General George McClellan had introduced his famous saddle (based, incidentally, on a Hungarian military version), troopers sat on a saddle not radically different from the stock saddles of the era. The McClellan of this period featured a center-fire rigging with a mohair cinch and hooded stirrups; the saddle itself had a split tree and raised pommel and cantle. The single, Hanoverian-type curb was in general use in the cavalry until well into the current century. Military and western horsemanship were not essentially dissimilar until the entire military system of equitation was overhauled by General Harry Chamberlain in the 1920s, primarily on Italian and French theories and techniques.

The gradual decline of the fork seat was largely the result of three factors: the change in the nature of cattle work, the improvement of the stock horse, and the influences of the rodeo arena. With the decline of large-scale cattle driving and the emergence of more or less modern conditions of ranch work, men on horseback spent more time sorting cattle than driving them and mounted on horses that contained far more "hot" blood, the ancestors of today's quarter horses. The influence of rodeo competition, a rapidly growing sport in the early years of the century, laid a heavy emphasis on speed, particularly in calf roping. These factors produced a sort of revolution in western riding—turning it back, incidentally, to a more Spanish style. It was awkward to ride a quick-moving stock horse employing the old fork seat; the high cantles and long fenders were unsuited to competitive roping. A new western form of riding, and the saddles that complemented it, appeared together, not long after the first world war. What had happened, in somewhat more technical terms, was that the principles of the "balanced" seat were beginning to be applied to western horsemanship. The shape of the saddle that emerged gives a clear picture of the changing style. The modern roping saddle sported a low cantle (for ease in dismounting), a low set front with narrow swells (allowing the rider to get directly over the horse's center of gravity at speed), fenders set further forward, and stirrups that permitted a much shorter adjustment. While many other styles of saddlery persisted—for rough work, breaking, and mountain riding—the roping saddle became a rather standard fixture, permitting, as it did, the use of a balanced-seat approach to horsemanship.

What was happening—perhaps unknown to many western horsemen—was that western horsemanship was moving back closer not only to its Spanish origins but also to the broad scientific principles that underlie all horsemanship. To judge the extent to which this is true today, you have only to read the American Horse Show Association's descriptions of the "ideal" positions that organization now sponsors for "Stock Seat" (western) and "Hunt Seat" (English) equitation. The essential principles of balance are largely similar, although there are, in fact, major differences in the two styles as regards other matters. Of course, if the old fork seat seems rather unscientific by contemporary standards, the methods of English riding of the same era are even more ludicrous, since they were based on theories now thoroughly repudiated. In 1904, an Italian cavalry captain by the name of Frederico Caprilli published a series of articles that shook the established theories of equitation. Caprilli proved, in essence, that the horse's center of gravity was not in the middle of his back (as was generally believed), but in the withers and that, as the horse increased the length of his stride, this center of gravity moved forward in the withers, from the rear to the front. With this modern "forward" riding, the English, or "International," style was born. But compare, if you like, the position of a rider jumping a fence (where the horse's center of gravity is in its most forward position) and a calf roper just leaving the box. You will discover very comparable positions, and for the very logical reason that both riders are anxious not to be "left behind," to be over the center of gravity of the horse.

Of course, good western horsemen were riding "balanced" long before they were introduced to more or less technical descriptions of it, sometimes by popularizers like Monte Foreman.[1] They were

---

[1] Monte Foreman in the period after World War II quite intelligently perceived that the principles of "classical" horsemanship, mainly expressed in elementary dressage work, were wholly applicable to western horsemanship. He popularized this concept in books and in his clinics; but he was not quite the pioneer some believe, since numerous western horsemen were sufficiently educated to realize the common foundation of equitation principles, and Mr. Foreman tended to create the impression that his methods were of his own devising, rather than being the quite conventional methods of classical riding.

17

doing so because the roots of western horsemanship go back to the earliest expressions of balanced riding, further, by the way, than the artificialities introduced by the *manege* horsemen of the seventeenth and eighteenth centuries.

The Western Horse

What is a "western horse"? Often that means simply a horse that carries a stock saddle on his back. The term "western horse," more accurately applied, refers in a historical sense to those horses—and, indeed, breeds of horses—that developed in the American West, principally in the last century. The two truly western breeds, in this sense, are the Quarter Horse and the Appaloosa, the former the result of the use of certain Thoroughbred strains in range mares, ultimately producing a standardized type, and the latter the curiously marked horses bred primarily by the Nez Perce Indians of the Northwest. Many other breeds "go western" exceptionally well, as in the case of the Arabian, the Morgan, the Thoroughbred, the Paint, or Pinto, even, occasionally, the American Saddlebred, but these breeds were developed elsewhere. The real western horse of the Old West was, of course, of less determinant origins, although his ancestry must trace to Spanish importations.

There were no horses native to North America prior to the Spanish explorations, and it is largely a myth that huge bands of wild (or, more properly, feral) horses roamed the western plains. The spread of the horse in the trans-Mississippi region was largely through trading and theft, although some escaped horses did reproduce and form bands of what the Spanish called *mustenyos* or "wild ones" (from which the Anglos derived the term "mustang"). The Indians bred horses, the Comanches and the Nez Perce were quite careful about this, even keeping breeding records. Large numbers of horses were introduced to the plains area—most of them representing the light horse breeds that had developed essentially from English stock, especially the Thoroughbred—by the great tide of westward settlement crossing the Mississippi Basin. These "Eastern-breds" were inevitably crossbred with the stock already there, descended from the original Spanish stock. The American Quarter Horse, today's

18

prototype of the western horse, was developed in this way. This process of attempting to combine the best features of the range horse (toughness, agility, endurance) with the qualities (speed, size, disposition) of the breeds of English origin, particularly the Thoroughbred and to a lesser extent the Morgan, formed the basis of the production of large numbers of horses suitable for military purposes. This basic breeding approach was maintained by the U.S. Cavalry until about the time of World War II. The need to upgrade for the purpose of providing cavalry remounts also affected the character of the horse used on the ranches of the West. The cow horse at the turn of the century looked a good deal different from wiry little mustang types typical at the close of the Civil War.

Horses bred west of the Mississippi obviously undertook many of the jobs that horses performed elsewhere; they carried people from place to place, pulled wagons and buggies, bore men to war, and took on a hundred agricultural chores, from herding cattle to propelling huge reapers. But the Great Plains of North America was one of the extraordinary horse-rearing regions of the world. It was ideal for both the use and reproduction of the horse; it was a "sea of grass" much like the seminal steppes of Eurasia. All the peoples who inhabited the plains came to develop, each in their own way, a "horse culture": the Spanish, the Indians, and the American frontiersmen. In this region, men felt more at home aboard a horse than they did on foot. When you stop to think about it, that era was one of absolutely unrivaled personal mobility, made possible by the relatively simple acquisition of horses.

The "sea of grass," itself conducive to the raising of horses, also encouraged particular forms of using the horse. The very size of the area and the nomadic character of the life it sponsored produced horses notable for endurance and toughness, much like the hardy ponies of the Mongols. The earliest use of the horse had been for war. The North American Indian quickly converted it for use as a hunting conveyance to chase buffalo, and the Anglo-Spanish cattlemen employed it for working the huge herds of livestock that the region could support. But all these uses stressed common qualities: toughness, mobility, docility, and speed from a quick acceleration.

The Indian prized his war and buffalo ponies above all else.

But, as the century wore on, the buffalo were gone and, after 1890, warfare, too, had come to an end. As the nineteenth century closed, the use of the horse for war by the now dominant white man was increasingly limited by the new technology. After chasing Pancho Villa around in 1916, the American cavalry would play no important mounted role in the Great War. The demand for remounts slackened; only one mounted division remained at the time of Pearl Harbor and it fought through the second world war almost entirely dismounted, as infantry. It was only as a working stock horse, then, that the horse of the West preserved its unique, environmentally induced qualities. No longer needed to carry soldiers or to pursue buffalo, the sturdy plains pony was still the indispensable tool of the stockman. The stock horse became the embodiment of the western horse.

In the post-Civil War West, the stock horse meant, as a rule, the small, wiry southern-plains range pony deriving from vaguely Spanish-Barb ancestry. Available in almost unlimited supply, it provided transportation for two generations of stockmen. Even in these early days, there was a good deal of specialization; some ponies were used for "cutting," others for trailing, still others for roping, riding fence, or working in rocky, hilly country. A drover's string usually contained an assortment of "specialists."

As a matter of fact, if the original stock horse was Spanish, trained in that singular style, the next version was the stock horse of the southern plains, influenced by the Spanish model, but emphasizing versatility and initiative. Yet a third major type emerged—the stock horse of the northern plains and mountain states, a beast quite different from his Texas-Oklahoma relation. The northern cow horse was an animal suited to the more rugged terrain of that region, a larger, sturdier horse, often carrying a strain of draft breeding. The three regional types of working cow horses are gone now, but traces of the styles that went with them remain. California and Arizona animals still show traces of the Spanish heritage; Texas and Oklahoma preserve some connections with the old southern cow pony; Montana and Idaho still fancy the rugged stock horse of their past.

But these styles had a great deal in common. The end was largely the same: to produce a quick-reining horse. The basic common denominator of all stock horses is reining ability, granted that rein on the roping horse is quite different from rein on a cutting horse. The stock horses of the final decades of the nineteenth century were breedier, larger, faster than the so-called "Spanish ponies" of a generation before, principally due to the increased use of pure-bred sires, particularly the Thoroughbred. Specialization continued to refine the stock horse, especially as rodeo and show competition tended to make their influences felt. Beyond "working cow horses," there appeared roping horses (that continue to this date to become even more specialized), cutting horses, and, eventually, "reining" horses used almost solely for competition in the show ring.

As the need for working stock on the range began to diminish after the first world war (due to several factors, but mostly significant changes in the procedures of the range cattle industry), the notion that the western stock horse might make a dandy horse for pleasure riding took hold, particularly when the mystique of the Old West was popularized by the advent of motion pictures.[2] The twin influences of rodeo and the movies not only broadened public appeal for the stock horse, but drastically changed many styles of western gear and clothing. The hero of the film western, more or less established on the screen by William S. Hart, was invariably accompanied by his faithful stock horse, with which he quite publicly shared his triumphs. Thus, the 1920s saw, among other cultural curiosities, the urge to relive the days of the Old West. Dude ranching became well established in this era, and the western horse no longer was restricted to the Great Plains or the country west of the Rockies. A new use had been found for the hardworking cow horse; he became a "pleasure" horse. Perhaps due to the influence of celluloid cowboys from Tom Mix to Roy Rogers, the stock horse often was "dolled up" to suit the flamboyant image of the "knight of the plains" with elaborate silver tack. Flashy horses like palominos, albinos, and blacks were fashionable; the "parade" horse became a new version of the western horse, still to be seen in gaudy array in events like the Rose Bowl Parade.

By the 1930s, the stock horse, who had long since begun earning his living in the rodeo arena, began also to appear in the

[2]After the earlier "peep show" productions of the Edison Company which used western subjects, *The Great Train Robbery* in 1903 was a "western." The popularity of "Bronco Billy" Anderson's films (1909–1919) helped establish the myth of the West, as did the shorter films of D.W. Griffith.

show ring. By the time of World War II, the present divisions of western show horses had become pretty well established: pleasure horses, trail horses, reining horses, and stock horses. This emphasis on the show ring was vigorously promoted by breed associations, particularly the American Quarter Horse Association, and by other breed groups that were beginning to feature western divisions in their horse shows, like the Arabians and Morgans. The post-World War II era also saw the firm establishment of other equestrian activities old in conception but only recently formalized into regulated sport, such as cutting and endurance and competitive trail riding. The National Cutting Horse Association, for illustration, was founded in 1946.

Most of these breed associations strongly endorsed a considerable emphasis on versatility (and also sponsored intense interest in conformation or "halter" competition). This versatility has grown markedly in scope. Today, the use of breeds like the Quarter Horse, the Appaloosa, the Arabian, and the Morgan is enthusiastically encouraged in traditionally English equipment as hunters, jumpers, bridle-path hacks, and even driving horses. Moreover, the popularity of racing certain western breeds, such as the Quarter Horse and the Appaloosa, stimulated by substantial prize monies, has had a significant effect on the development of these breeds, sometimes tending to develop the breed away from the qualities most functional in stock horses. In the case of the Quarter Horse (surely the most successful of the more recent breeds), the emphasis on racing meant the wholesale use of Thoroughbred blood to enhance running capability. While tracing its ancestry to the Thoroughbred in the first place, the modern Quarter Horse is the result of recent direct influences of such foundational Thoroughbred sires as *Three Bars, Depth Charge,* and *Top Deck,* among others. Additional doses of Thoroughbred blood potentially jeopardized the utilitarian charactistics of the breed, moving it away from the stock-horse model. For a time in the very recent past, it appeared that two distinct types of Quarter Horses would emerge: an "arena" type (more or less resembling the original stock-horse prototype) and a "running" type (closely approximating the Thoroughbred in conformation and disposition). Fortunately, perceptive Quarter Horse breeders appreciated this risk and are currently breeding to a common standard, although certainly Quarter Horses are much larger than in the past. Some improvement, too, has resulted from the close-up Thoroughbred connection: better wither definition, better pasterns, and better front angulation.

Most of the other more-or-less western breeds (the Appaloosa, the Paints and Pintos, the Buckskins, and others) have undergone very real problems in standardizing type. In recent years, these breeds have strongly tended to accept the Quarter Horse conformation standard—at least in the show ring, although their official breed descriptions often appear at variance with this. The Appaloosa breed standard, for example, describes a horse distinctly different from the Quarter Horse, but most winning "Appys" in the ring closely resemble Quarter Horses at the present time. Of course, many of these breeds are constituted on the basis of color or markings (although the Appaloosa has a substantial claim to a historically verifiable type), and on this basis conformation standards are difficult to establish. In the past few years, there has been a great proliferation of breed associations, including such exotic groups as the American Mustang Association, the Indian Horse Association, and the Half-Bred Registry, all of somewhat doubtful historical validity.

What Is the Western Horse?

If it is no longer practical to describe or define the "western horse" in terms of breed or type, it is logical to designate western horses as those trained in the techniques of western horsemastership, irrespective of their historical origins. Despite the wide versatility in the uses of western horses and the promotional efforts of breed associations to advertise their "all-purpose" capabilities, the western horse remains essentially a stock horse, a horse trained along the lines of traditional stock-horse methods. The system of training and riding identifiable as the "western" method rests on objectives shaped in the development of working stock horses. This is not as narrow a base as it might seem if it is remembered that the stock horse was a direct lineal emanation from the war and hunting horses of the ancient past. The point to be made is that the western horse and the western method that produces him has a *utilitarian* objective; the western horse is a working animal, even if today he is most frequently used for

23

recreational purposes, for pleasure or competition in equestrian games.

The stock horse, in its development, has been characterized by four main qualities: hardiness, agility, docility, and a fourth factor, less tangible, that is usually called "cow sense" or, simply, "cow."

Hardiness is necessary in any working animal. The stock horse is bred to take it. The demands made on a working stock horse or on a competitive horse are considerable in terms of physical and mental stress and strain. He must carry a good deal of weight, often for long periods and in rough country, while performing hard, often jolting work. A roping horse, for example, has to be able to stay on his feet against the shock of a roped calf or steer. That is why stock horses, although not usually tall, are heavily built and powerful. A 14.2 Quarter Horse may weigh twelve hundred pounds. Stock horses cannot be delicate or prone to unsoundness; they must have a tough resilience and what a horseman calls "bottom."

Agility is a quality not restricted to stock horses. Other obvious examples of agile horses are polo ponies and those remarkable *rejoneo* horses of Spain and Portugal that are used in the mounted passing of the bull in the *corrida*.[3] Dressage horses are also agile in their way. Agility is the result of the development of balance and suppleness, both qualities in part the result of conformation. The stock horse, therefore, is a close-coupled, short-backed horse with a relatively short leg, a strongly developed haunch, and a good deal of front angulation. Generally speaking, the stock horse travels low at his gaits without much elevation of the knee and hocks (in contrast, say, to gaited horses or Hackneys). His natural head carriage is low, but he must possess sufficient refinement of the head and neck to permit the "flexing" necessary to attain balance.

These "beauties" of conformation enable the stock horse, when properly trained, to maneuver easily at speed, to stop and start quickly and economically, to accelerate swiftly, and to move with

---

[3] These are not to be confused with the poor "skates" that the picadors sit on. These *rejoneos*, superbly trained Andalusian horses, participate in the working of the bulls by speed and maneuver. Many of the *Charro* games in Mexico employ horses with equal talents and training.

a minimim of waste effort. This quality of agility, vital to a working stock horse or a roping or cutting horse, permits a way of going, a smoothly balanced set of gaits, that also makes him a comfortable, pleasurable ride.

Docility, a quiet, tractable disposition, is a prime characteristic of the stock horse, the "bucking bronco" image of the western horse notwithstanding. It is true enough that in the old days there were some pretty salty stock horses, but this was due in the main to quick methods of breaking and the mixed ancestries of many of the animals. Ranchers soon discovered, though, that these erratic horses wasted time and energy and that horses with sound dispositions, properly "broken," were a practical necessity. The fact of the matter is that a placid disposition is more or less indispensable in the horse that works. The stock horse must be used; little attention can be paid to constantly managing him and, therefore, a horse that is calm and businesslike is all-important. The temperament of a good stock horse is rather phlegmatic; he does what he's asked, but he doesn't volunteer any spontaneous bursts of energy or temper. The stock horse is not "spirited," using that horrible word that people who don't know much about horses are so fond of employing.

When you talk about *cow sense,* you're likely talking about genetic factors. Horses are born with cow sense; they don't acquire it, except in the sense that their innate instincts are tempered, refined, and enhanced. Most horses, incidentally, seem to enjoy working cattle, and doing so is beneficial for any horse. But some horses have a special knack for it—which is what makes champion cutting and reined cow horses. Most western horses never see a cow these days, I suppose, but cow sense is still one of the qualities of a good stock horse, and all western horses retain their stock-horse ancestry.

But the term "stock horse" is, in a manner of speaking, a generic term. In the age of specialization, the term may be more precisely applied to a specialized type of horse actually working cattle or competing in classes requiring cattle work. These horses are frequently called "reined cow horses." In competition, these horses work both "dry" reining patterns and also exhibit their skill in moving and controlling cattle.

Cutting horses are rather extreme equine specialists, the

Cadillacs of the stock horses. Aside from actual ranch work in sorting cattle (done quite differently from cutting horse competitions, by the way), cutting horses engage in an equestrian game that requires them to separate individual cattle from a small herd and then prevent the isolated steer from rejoining the herd. Cutting horses, unlike any other equine performers, are asked to work without any cues or guidance from the rider once the horse is put down on the "cut" steer.

Reining horses are athletic animals that compete by running "reining patterns" that usually require figure eights, "roll backs," spins, and quick stops, some of these movements at speed. In theory, reining horses show those qualities of agility needed in a working stock horse, but most reining horses do not have actual live experience with stock, although competitive reining horses usually profit from some exposure to cattle work.

Trail horses come in a number of variations. The trail horses seen at horse shows are judged on their ability to negotiate a series of artificial obstacles or tests designed to show their steadiness and handiness, their general usefulness as pleasant and safe conveyances on the trail. They are also asked, in the show ring, to "work the rail" as pleasure horses. Competitive trail riding, as a sport, involves cross-country riding over varied terrain in which the horse's condition is evaluated, as well as his ability to complete the ride. Endurance riding is a competition involving longer distances in which the order of finish is the primary means of judgment. Of course, many trail horses are actually trail horses, used for pleasure riding cross-country or as mounts for hunters, fishermen, and those who like to explore remote and otherwise inaccessible country. Trail horses are tough, quiet, and surefooted.

Pleasure horses include the bulk of all western horses. The term "pleasure horse" can be applied to both the well-manicured show-ring contestants and to "backyard" horses used purely for recreation of a more casual sort. Pleasure horses of all types should have faultless manners, attractive gaits, and, hopefully, a handsome appearance. They are not expected to have a "quick rein" like a competitive stock horse but nonetheless they should be agile and reasonably prompt. Some also double as trail horses. In the show ring, a pleasure horse is shown at the walk, jog, and lope (and may be asked to extend the latter two gaits) on a light rein with both manners and extreme smoothness of gaits. They should back quietly and straight. They are also judged on suitability to the rider and on general appearance.

Another category might be the "equitation" horse, or horses used to mount junior riders in a variety of equitation or horsemanship classes that are judged on the basis of the rider's performance. While the horse presumably is not judged, the show ring junior competitors in these classes cannot expect much success unless they're mounted on horses more or less carefully trained for this sort of competition. Frequently pleasure horses also serve as equitation horses, although some equitation classes demand a horse that reins faster than the average pleasure horse.

Roping horses constitute another example of specialization, not only in the sense that they are used exclusively for roping competition, but in regard to the particular types of roping done. There are "calf roping" horses, "steer roping" horses, and "team roping" horses—and this last category is subdivided into horses that specialize in "heading" and "heeling." A good roping horse has exceptional speed from a standing position, an ability to put the rope in close to his target, a quick stop, and the capacity to work the rope.

Dogging horses are creatures of the rodeo arena used in the "bulldogging" event. Like roping horses, they must be speedy, obedient, and able to take the contestant tight against the steer.

Another major classification is made up of horses used for various equestrian competitions called "gymkhanas" or, occasionally, "gaming." The most familiar animals of this type are "barrel" horses used in running cloverleaf barrel patterns at speed against the clock (the only professionally sanctioned rodeo event for women). Other popular "game" events are pole-bending, the "keyhole race," the "stump race," goat-typing, and a host of others too numerous to list. The Appaloosa Horse Club, in particular, formally sanctions a wide variety of this sort of event in its regular horse shows. In some areas, "cowboy polo" is a mounted game with a considerable following.[4]

These are only the main specializations that western horses are currently undertaking. Western-trained horses are a fixture at

[4]Western-trained horses are frequently converted for use in regular polo (which is played in English tack) since some of the training of the polo pony is similar to that of a reining horse.

racetracks as lead ponies. Some police organizations use western-trained horses. Various mounted patrols—some of them involved in serious search-and-rescue operations—use western horses. Western drill teams and parade groups are common. By the way, most of the jobs performed by horses can be duplicated by mules. The mule is becoming increasingly popular in the Southwest as a trail and pleasure mount, and horse shows are featuring, more and more, classes for mules. Bishop, California, now boasts an annual mule show drawing hundreds of exhibitors, virtually reproducing the range of classes presented at horse shows.

The qualities and characteristics instilled by stock-horse training and the techniques of western horsemanship produce horses that have a wide and increasing appeal for the recreationally oriented public. There are, I believe, several reasons for this popularity of the western horse, some obvious, some more subtle.

A part of this appeal can be attributed to the fact that the western horse is a part of our history; it is, in a sense, an American heritage. Popular literature extols not only the "cowboy" but also the cow horse. Western-style riding does not suffer from some of the social overtones of English horsemanship that is (quite unfairly) often identified with excessive formality, class distinctions, and even a certain amount of snobbery. It is interesting to note that English riding tends, in this country, to be quite female dominated in terms of the proportion of students and horse-show exhibitors, especially among the young. This is not true of the western style, where men and boys hold their own, numerically speaking. Western riding is very adaptable to the broadest range of physical abilities, talents, motivations, and even ages and sizes. Western horsemanship sponsors a certain self-reliance, individuality, and a sense of excitement and freedom that is not wholly unique by any means, but is very pronounced, nonetheless. The western horse stays pretty close to nature; it generally avoids the artificialities that encumber some other types of horses. Western horses are usually well cared for, but they are not babied or pampered. Finally, the western horse offers the potentiality for truly artistic horsemanship, comparable to any form of the so-called equestrian "disciplines." I have a rather extensive familiarity with the riding and training of jumpers, hunters, combined training and dressage horses, and I am convinced without a doubt that the riding and training of the stock horse demands a finesse, a discipline, a cultivation of equestrian skill equal to any other form of horsemanship and combines with this an excitement and an aesthetic appeal correspondingly intense.

The Aims of Western Horsemanship

The history of western horsemanship reveals that riding the horse has not been an end in itself. The techniques of riding are devoted to the efficiency with which the horse performs certain tasks. The horse, in one sense, becomes an implement, often a working tool, and, in another sense, an extension of the rider's will—that will concerned almost wholly with the job at hand. This last point deserves more explanation. In all forms of riding, the training of the rider involves two elements: the training of the mind—that is, the conscious awareness of what the rider ought to do; the training of the subconscious responses—the immediate "stimulus-and-response" mechanisms where the rider reacts by habitual conditioning rather than from deliberation. The analogy I often use to describe this is taken from the sport of fencing. If you have to decide which parry you're going to use to counter a lunge, you're already run through! The hand must be quicker than the conscious mind.

In western riding this second element is particularly important, because in order to "use" the horse, to make it an instant vehicle of your intentions, you have to learn to ride with a relatively small degree of direct consciousness of what you're doing. The ultimate aim is to make the horse a sort of four-footed extension of your body. If I want to gallop down to the far end of the arena to talk to somebody, I don't consciously make a decision as to how I'm going to use the aids or what position I ought to be in when the horse steps into the lope. I just go there, spontaneously and efficiently. The first objective, then, of western horsemanship is this level of instant, consciously unmeditated, technique—to *think* what you *want* to do is virtually to do it.

In order to accomplish this, the relationship of horse and rider is one of intense *intimacy*. The horse and rider are always together, the rider is never operating *against* the horse—which a rider may do, quite legitimately, in some other forms of equita-

29

tion. For example, only in instances of the full extension of the galloping stride does the western rider leave his intimate contact with the horse's spine. Occasionally, for one reason or another, the western rider may ask his horse to extend the trot from the customary "jog" (slow, short trot), and he may, therefore, "post" (rise off the saddle on the alternate beats or "diagonals" of the trot) or even stand in his stirrups, but the general position of the western rider at the trot is in contact with the seat of the saddle—although, as we shall see, not with all his weight there. Or another illustration: the bit and reins in western horsemanship are almost never used as a means of exerting continuous physical restraint, actually displacing the movements of the horse by hand pressure (as is commonly done in other forms of riding). The western rider, then, is not operating *against* the horse, but *with* it; he is cueing, rather than restraining. The impulse of the rider and the horse must be one, and this unity is based upon the high degree of intimacy that this form of riding introduces.

The fundamental aim of western horsemanship, when all is said and done, is the ability to *maneuver the horse at speed.* All forms of equitation are somewhat similar at the level of walk-trot-gallop around a ring, but beyond this sort of activity the emphasis shifts to more specific and diversified abilities; in the "hunt seat," for instance, the obvious objective is to jump obstacles effectively. In western riding, that advanced emphasis is on being able to work a horse in demanding patterns of movement at considerable speed. Nearly all forms of western riding competition (essentially those with a stock-horse base) require this in one way or another. Even the show-ring pleasure horse, working at the slowest variations of the jog and lope, must convey the impression (provided by his balance and responsiveness) of being able to be "turned on" instantly by the rider. The ability to maneuver at speed is augmented by the capability of horse and rider to switch this speed on and off with ease, to stop and start with calm precision.

All of the above objectives ought to be met with the maximum degree of *comfort* to both horse and rider. No form of serious horsemanship is ever wholly natural; often our untrained instincts are not correct guides. But western riding, based on its utilitarian traditions of the horse as a working tool, emphasizes a very considerable degree of naturalness, to the extent that often when the rider *feels* comfortable, he is likely doing what he ought to.

The customary gaits of the western horse are rooted in maximizing comfort. Western equipment (saddles, bridles, blankets) was developed as a response both to practical needs and to the demands of comfort, since it was assumed that the western horseman would spend long, active hours in the saddle. Try spending long hours in a so-called "close contact" jumping saddle or a Lane Fox-type gaited horse saddle and you will appreciate the difference, the factor of comfort in a stock saddle.

Western horsemanship is pragmatic; it tends to place more emphasis on results than on forms or means. It is flexible (within reasonable limits). It does not stress correctness for its own sake, unless it's related to improving performance. This does *not* mean that western horsemanship is sloppy or careless or anti-theoretical; witness the rigor of performance standards. Like all really excellent horsemanship, the western style is at its best when it *appears* simple. That easy naturalness is really the outgrowth of dedicated, disciplined work, but the end product ought to be the picture of simplicity, even a sort of casual effortlessness. If this is true of the rider, incidentally, it is also true of the horse. The well-trained horse-and-rider combination should never appear "busy," as if both partners were putting out all they could manage. Perhaps the hard-bitten cowhand would shudder at being called graceful, but, in fact, that is the vivid impression created by the accomplished western horseman.

We have been discussing the aims or objectives of western horsemanship, what it ought to be like. Now it's time to face the problem of "means." How do you start, progress from being barely able to buckle on a halter to being able to work a stock horse with that gracefulness suggested above? To do that, you have to take a deep breath and, in the next chapter, "put your foot in the stirrup."

2

Putting Your
Foot in the Stirrup

By way of introduction, his name is *equus caballus* in scientific circles—the horse. Introductions are in order, because so many beginning riding students these days have never really met a horse before. Having never been on intimate terms, most "green," neophyte horsemen don't know very much about the beast they propose to work with and ride. Most people who make their first acquaintance with the horse in a lesson situation have a flock of erroneous ideas about the horse's character. As a rule, beginners either think the horse resembles a machine, like all the others they're used to, or they suspect that the horse is lying in wait for them, full of evil, aggressive designs. Of course the horse isn't a machine, it's an animate being with a distinct, individual personality, with likes and dislikes. But a well-trained horse is also a creature of habit, so all these "personal" variations of behavior have a limited range and the horse performs mostly from habitual responses and relatively little from spontaneous volition.

The horse is not, of course, just standing there, sizing up the student, planning how best to discomfort him. In the first place, the horse, like all grazing animals that have for centuries been wary of predators, is essentially timid and flight is its only real defense. That doesn't mean that the trained horse is always quaking in fear, but he is certainly not aggressive, either. Only rarely do you see a horse that displays signs of an innately aggressive disposition; horses with such unpleasant traits are almost invariably made that way by bad handling.

The horse also is not very intelligent. Whatever else may be his virtues, brains are not among them. The old expression "horse sense" is very suspect. Even rated against other common domestic animals, the horse achieves a poor score on the intelligence scale. A man *should,* incidentally, be able to out-think a horse—but I've seen a few fellows out-guessed from time to time. Because a horse has a limited intelligence, his outlook on the world, his range of thought, is decidedly restricted. He does not really try to out-scheme you. Generally the problem is one of communication. The horse is willing, most of the time, to do what you want; the question is to transmit your wishes to him in a way he can assimilate. Balky, rebellious horses are usually animals whose resistance has come about from being mismanaged, acquiring regrettable defensive habits. Horses are trained, by the way, in a manner directly opposite from training a more mentally complicated animal like the dog. Dogs are trained by reward, by "positive reinforcement," as the psychologists would put it; the dog responds, his behavior is modified, by his desire for praise or the reward of some tidbit. The horse, conversely, is trained by "negative reinforcement": a mildly painful sensation is relieved when the horse obeys the rider's direction—as in the case of the bit, for example. The horse is "rewarded" by the elimination of an unpleasant sensation. He has no capacity (or very little) to relate a positive reward to his own actions; you can pat a horse on the neck and say "good boy" until the cows come home, but it won't mean anything to him.[1] Further, he has no desire to please you, unlike a dog; he obeys because he has found a security (from his natural timidity) in habits he has acquired and with which he has come to associate an absence of unpleasant sensations. The intelligence range among horses is correspondingly narrow. I

[1] Despite all the tales of literature to the contrary, the horse has no real affection for human beings. That is outside his emotional range. He may prefer one person to another, but this is the result of his feelings of greater confidence in one than in the other. A horse may have a certain "security blanket" relationship with a particular man or woman, but this is not a case of actual affection or loyalty, as in the case of a dog.

have worked "bright" horses and "stupid" horses—there are signs of intelligence like problem-solving that can give you hints about this—but the differences are not all that great. Nor is greater intelligence necessarily an asset in a performance horse. As cases in point, I think cutting horses have to have a relatively high level of intelligence (for horses) and roping horses ought not to be too bright, comparatively speaking.

Getting to know the horse you're going to learn on (as a sort of representative of the whole species) is a necessary first step to riding it. This kind of rather primitive familiarity is mostly tactile; it involves touching, handling the animal. Grooming is a good way, as is any other association with the horse that features getting close to it. I usually start by having beginners simply lead the horse on foot for a short time to accustom them to being close to a horse and moving around it. Almost from the start, the beginner ought to learn to "tack" the horse himself, put the gear on. Saddling is not only an obviously necessary function, but it is also a means of commencing a knowledge of horsemastership, of developing a feel for dealing with horses.

Walking a horse around a little before you mount is a good idea, even after you've become an experienced rider. This preliminary walk helps to ease the saddle and other gear into place before you get aboard. Starting out, it's sensible to lead the horse into the ring or arena and mount him there. Later, you can ride back and forth from the barn.

Putting on the Tack

There are a few tips I'd pass along about saddling that are often neglected.

The first suggestion I'd make about putting on the tack is simply not to be in a hurry. Take your time. Don't throw it up on the horse as if the barn was on fire. Pass the saddle blanket a couple of times over the horse's back before setting the saddle on; it helps smooth down the hairs of the back. I like to use both a blanket and a "hair pad" under the saddle. Many inexperienced people tend to set the saddle too far back. Make sure the leading edge of the saddle is well up on the top end of the horse's shoulders. Before cinching up, wiggle the saddle a little to make sure its "bars" are in a comfortable relationship with the withers. Don't cinch the horse too rapidly. Take your time and gradually tighten it—you may have to tighten it more than once. You want a cinch to be snug, not only because you don't want the saddle to slip, but also because a loose cinch may give a horse a girth gall (an abrasion of the skin under the cinch). There is some sense in using a sheepskin cinch cover, by the way, to put your mind to rest about galls. If you're using a back cinch as well, buckle it up enough so that it doesn't hang down to the place where a horse could put a foot in it. Except for roping or mountain riding, there is little need to actually tighten the back cinch on a "double rig." Oh, and do loop the near-side latigo back through the saddle dee and tie up the off-side rigging on a saddlestring or the rope-hanger; that way you won't trip carrying the saddle and you'll keep your rigging a lot cleaner.

The western bridle, happily, is a simple piece of gear. There isn't much to putting it on and taking it off. I will only mention a few useful hints. When removing the bridle, be careful not to let the bit hit the front teeth of the horse. Lower it slowly. Horses resent having their teeth banged in this way. On very cold days, you might warm the mouthpiece of the bit with your hand before presenting it to the horse. It is surprising how many bridles you see that are not properly adjusted. Adjust the headstall so that the curb bit fits smoothly but not too tightly in the corners of the horse's mouth. It should not hang down. With a snaffle, the adjustment should be a little snugger, so that a wrinkle appears at the corner of the mouth. Adjust the curb strap or chain so that the strap will engage against the lower jaw when the shanks of the bit are at right angles to the lips of the horse. This is a general rule of thumb, of course, and there are valid reasons, from time to time, for altering this adjustment.

Mounting and Dismounting

There are a lot of ways to get on a horse. It's traditional, for example, to mount the horse from the left or "near" side. You are on the near side, by the way, if the horse's head is on your left side. But there is really no reason why you couldn't mount from the right or "off" side; Indians used to, the Chinese cavalry does, and calf ropers will get off a horse on the side closest to the calf. But horses get used to being "fooled with" on the near side; they're led, saddled, mounted from that side and most people start to groom them on the near side, too.

Westerners, being individualists at heart, have evolved a number of ways of mounting. Who can say which is correct? There are, though, two easy, safe, and very orthodox ways to get on a western horse that I would recommend. Try both and decide which one suits you.

The first method, favored by people who ride a lot of "green" stock, involves standing at the horse's left shoulder, facing the animal's rear, reins gathered relatively short in the left hand. With the free right hand, turn the left stirrup toward you and put your left foot in it. Then hop gently on your right leg so that you move to a right angle to the horse. You can then take your right hand and get a grip on *either* the cantle (the back of the saddle) or the pommel (the horn or the swells), but it is customary among westerners *not* to touch the cantle when mounting. For ordinary riding, there is no particular reason for this custom, but if you're sensitive about being thought a "dude," you'd better take your hold on the pommel. Having done this, push down on your right foot, almost making a little jump, and swing the right leg over the back of the saddle and lightly let the body settle gently into the saddle. Pick up your stirrup on the off side with the right foot. Don't just plump your weight down on the horse's back; its kidneys are located behind the cantle and it doesn't appreciate having your bulk banged down on them. The main advantage of this method of mounting is that *if* the horse were to move forward suddenly, its motion would tend to swing you up in the saddle—assuming that your control of the reins didn't prevent this from happening. In any form of mounting, keep the reins in the left hand short enough to hold the horse stationary. It's very annoying to have a horse move forward while you're trying to mount, and it's a bad habit you ought to discourage firmly.

The alternative method is sometimes called the Texas or Oklahoma "Hop," almost universally used by ropers, among others. In some ways, it's a little more elegant than the first technique. To do it, stand close to the horse's left side facing its head with, of course, the reins short in the left hand. Put the left foot in the stirrup and then reach forward and grasp the pommel

Mounting facing the head. The reins are held short, but not applying tension. Stand close to the horse, and push off with the right leg.

Mounting facing the tail. This is a useful way of mounting green or unreliable horses. The rider will come to right angles to the saddle and then swing aboard.

with the right hand. Give a hop off the right foot and swing up, helped by the slight pull you get from your grip on the horn or swells. Some people think it's dashing to jump into the stirrup with the left foot and swing up in one motion. There are those who even vault into the saddle without using the stirrup at all. I discourage these athletic feats, because the main objective in mounting is the comfort of the horse and mounting should be done, therefore, quietly, even slowly. The body should always be lowered gently into the saddle.

Dismounting is comparatively simple. Put your right hand on the horn and disengage your right foot from the stirrup. Lean slightly forward, putting your weight into the left stirrup, and then swing the right leg over the back of the saddle, allowing it, finally, to make contact with the ground. When the right foot is on terra firma, release your hold on the horn, slip the left foot out of the stirrup, and you will have, gracefully, we hope, dismounted. Like nearly everything else connected with horsemanship, practice will give you an easy familiarity with mounting and dismounting—to the point where you won't even think about it at all.

Have you ever marveled at how easily the hero of western movies mounts? The trick to this, they tell me, is that often the left stirrup is lowered way down to assist the process. I don't recommend this; it's awkward or impossible to readjust stirrup lengths in a stock saddle while sitting in it. But don't try to mount if you know that the stirrups are excessively short, far shorter than you'll want when mounted. It is hard to judge correct stirrup adjustment from the ground. Once mounted, the best way to get at least a preliminary stirrup adjustment is to sit where you belong, in the deepest part of the saddle, and let the legs fall naturally along the sides of the horse, feet out of the stirrups. With the legs in this position, the tread of the stirrup (the part against which the foot rests) should hit slightly below the rider's ankle joint. This is a rule of thumb, not an exact measurement, for two reasons: first, stirrup lengths will depend to some extent on the rider's individual body conformation and, second, stirrup lengths vary in accordance with certain forms of riding. Cutting-horse riders generally use a longer stirrup than ropers do, for example. Proper stirrup adjustment is extremely important. There is a prevalent fallacy that westerners invariably ride with very long stirrups; this is a holdover, possibly, from the days of the fork seat, I suppose. The stirrup adjustment is designed to bring a considerable amount of weight into the stirrup. Over-long stirrups prevent this, while over-short stirrups push the rider's lower body out of its position in the dip of the saddle, forcing the trunk against the cantle. You should never have to feel that you're reaching for the stirrups. But stirrups that are too short will not only spoil your position, but will also cramp your knees; and for this reason, on long rides where the pace is slow, most riders lower their stirrups. Try the simple form of measurement suggested above and then adjust stirrups up and down, based on other relevant factors. One more word about stirrup length: the holes in the stirrup leathers of western saddles are often quite far apart, making precise adjustment difficult. You can always use a leather punch and make sets of new holes between the pre-existing ones. But measure the holes you want to punch out with some care so that they are even on both sides and also will fit the "quick-change" buckles.

Holding the Reins

Like mounting, there are a number of options when it comes to holding the reins. Of course, western horsemanship usually involves holding the reins in one hand, although there are some instances in which so-called "squaw-reining" (holding the reins in two hands and direct reining) is used, such as operating the bosal hackamore and, needless to say, in training horses not yet schooled to the curb bit and the neck rein. But for ordinary equitation, the grip is with one hand. Either hand can be used, but if you are normally right-handed you would carry the reins in your left hand, and vice versa. In the show ring, you can ride with either hand, but you must not switch hands during the class.

In picking up the reins, it is necessary to consider both how to hold them and how to adjust their length. In holding the reins, I'd suggest you choose between two well-accepted forms (although I'm much more partial to the first one, frankly). This first alternative is used by virtually all reining-horse riders. Place your index finger between the reins, the "extra" length of rein crossing the face of the fingers or palm of the hand and falling below the little finger. The excess part of the rein should be carried on the

39

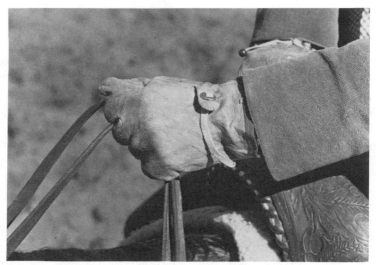

The preferred rein grip. Notice that the reins are held toward the ends of the fingers. The hand is at an angle of about forty-five degrees to the horse's neck. The wrist is straight and relaxed.

The optional rein grip. This is a less popular hold. The palm of the hand is held in a relatively flat position.

near side of the horse. The hand itself should be about half-closed, the reins carried between the first and second joints of the index finger. The advantage of this hold is that it is highly sensitive, allowing use of the fingers and the quick intervention of the wrist.

Your other choice is to bring the hand down on top of the reins, allowing each rein to separately pass through the fingers (usually one rein between the little and ring finger and another between the middle and index finger), the remaining length of rein coming out between the index finger and the thumb. In this grip, the palm of the hand tends to be carried flat. The excess or "bight" of the rein is allowed to fall on the off side of the horse. This method could be called the "military" or "polo" grip, and it is a comfortable way to carry the reins, particularly if, for some reason, you're using four reins instead of two—as you might for training use separate reins from a hackamore and a snaffle.

The best way to pick up the reins is to allow them first to be fully slack. Gradually shorten them until you can actually feel the horse's mouth, and then allow the hand itself to move forward an inch or two. In ordinary equitation, the hand is carried slightly in front of and slightly above the saddle horn. The western horse works on both the slack rein with no contact at all, or a very light contact, a "floating" rein. The reins, then, should be light, having a featherweight contact with the mouth, since they are used more for cueing than restraining. The hand itself should be virtually limp, never rigid or strained. Hold the reins as if you were clutching a piece of fine china.

Moving Out

So far you've managed to mount, have properly adjusted stirrups, and can hold the reins correctly. What next? The best thing to do is to simply walk the horse along the rail for a while to get used to the feel of the saddle and the motion of the horse under you. To get to the rail, just point your horse's head in that direction any way you can and squeeze him a little with your legs. You will notice immediately that even your perception of the world around you changes when you're in the saddle; from the horse's back, you're looking at the landscape from a different

A successful riding lesson begins with a clear understanding between student and instructor about the objectives of the session and the techniques to be used.

angle. Nothing has been said yet about how you should sit or how you should get the horse to move or change direction. As a matter of fact, you've gotten to the "track" by something other than polished skill. The word "track" is worth a note. Assuming that you're in a ring or an arena (and you must be, because you can't learn to ride without working in some kind of an enclosure to help you), the track is that area immediately alongside the ring fence or arena wall. This track is your primary working area during instruction; keep the horse moving ahead straight on the track during the early phases of learning to ride. It is good discipline for both the horse and the rider to keep consistently on the track, going deep into the corners of the ring.

You may notice as you're walking along that the horse nods its head at the walk. The walk is a four-beat gait and the horse consistently nods its head as it moves ahead. In western riding, the extremely light contact you have with the mouth makes it unnecessary for you to move your hand at the walk. It can stay entirely still. If, however, you increased that contact (as in English riding, by the way), it would be necessary for you to yield the hand back and forth in order to keep the bit pressure

42

constant. I mention this only to reiterate how important it is to preserve that *extremely* light contact so as to allow the horse to walk forward freely and boldly, not interfering with the motion of its head. The French have a proverb that says the "walk is the mother of the gaits," and it is true. Later, we shall pay some attention to encouraging the best possible walk, but for now you must only take care not to tighten the reins due to the unaccustomed motion of the horse. Very frequently, western horses are walked on an entirely slack rein.

Relax and let the horse move quietly on the track, making sure your hand on the rein is limp and flexible, also the wrist and forearm. Let your free hand and arm hang loose, or rest the hand against your thigh. Let the body itself be free of tension and find the deepest part of the saddle with the lower body.

Building the Position

Now that you've toured the ring and have become familiar with it, as well as with the novel sensation of sitting on a moving horse, it is time to tackle the basic position of the rider insofar as the walk and halt are concerned. The best way to do this is to start with the feet in the stirrups and work upward.

The basic position. Notice the deep heel position, the legs under the body in support, the buttocks pushed back against the cantle, and the back slightly arched but not stiff. The hand and wrist are limp and responsive. The impression of balance is unmistakable.

LEGS AND FEET

Place the widest part of the foot—about where the toes join the main part—against the tread of the stirrup. If you place more of your foot into the stirrup, it will be hard to bend the ankle; if you put less of your foot in, you won't have much weight against the tread and, consequently, little security.

The toe of your boot ought to turn out slightly, about 15–20 degrees, if you want to be more precise. If you don't turn them out at all (or even turn them in), you won't be able to bring the calf and lower thighs of the leg against the middle of the horse, and those muscles supply a certain amount of grip. If you turn them out too much, you will disengage the leg, even the knee. Riding is a matter predominantly of *balance*—of the relationship of the rider's weight to the center of gravity of the horse—but leg grip is a secondary source of support. The stock saddle with its wide, thick fenders and substantial rigging does not offer the possibilities for leg grip that the English or "flat" saddle does, but, despite this limitation, the ability to bring as much of the leg as possible in against the barrel of the horse is significant.

Since balance is the key, the principal means of getting it is to use the stirrups as the base of that balance, and this means bringing weight into the stirrups so as not to place the rider's entire weight on the horse's back, thus making the rider vulnerable, by the way, to sudden, unexpected shifts in the horse's haunches. I am not suggesting "standing in the stirrups" at all; the rider is fully seated, there is weight against the horse's spine, but there is also considerable weight supported directly in the stirrups. The legs kept *under* the body and weight placed into the stirrups gives the rider the capability of remaining in balance as the horse changes gait and direction.

The heel is lowered as far as possible, largely by bending the ankle joint. This is usually somewhat difficult for a beginner, but *all else depends on it,* for unless the heel is kept consistently in this position, weight cannot be brought against the stirrup tread. Without that weight, the stirrup can slip off the foot. It is not natural to hold the ankle in this position, and you cannot expect to keep your heels down all the time at the beginning. Your ankles may feel cramped, and if they do you can take your feet out of the stirrups for a few minutes and rotate your ankles. Ultimately, the whole leg, from the hip joint down, should not

44

move, but this cannot be accomplished immediately. For a while the lower leg will swing a little, due to your not yet complete balance and a lack of muscle tone.[2] Be patient, but concentrate hard on keeping the heels down.

Proper stirrup adjustment should create a reasonable bend of the leg at the knee. One of the old saws of riding is, "Grip with your knees." Don't. And don't allow your knees to stiffen or grow tense. Hold them firm enough so they won't move back and forth, but the knee is not a good gripping surface and if you squeeze hard with your knees the effect will be to disengage the lower leg and even to cause the heels to come up.

The line of the leg ought to follow approximately along the rear edge of the cinch, the leg very distinctly *under* the rider's body. If you look down at your kneecaps, you should be able to see only a small tip of your boot protruding. A very common fault in western equitation is to allow the legs to go forward toward the horse's shoulders, the legs out in front of the weight of the rider— having the feet "on the dashboard." This causes the body to move back against the cantle and real balance is lost. On the other hand, if the heels come up and the legs are drawn back behind the line of the cinch, then the rider goes onto his knees, is tilted forward, and his "sitting bones" lose contact with the saddle. That may be a good attitude for prayer, but not for riding.

[2]There are really no dismounted exercises that help much in tightening the leg muscles. The best and quickest way to firm up these muscles is to ride without stirrups at the slow trot for fairly lengthy periods. Riding bareback is not recommended. Prolonged riding without the saddle and stirrups tends to cause the rider to gain the missing balance by using the reins for balance, hanging on the horse's mouth. It is virtually impossible to ride bareback without taking an excessive hold on the mouth, and a great deal of bareback riding will definitely coarsen the hands. All the skill of the hands depends on the security of the seat. Without a secure seat, the hands are "handcuffed" and cannot work independently of the rest of the body.

THE LOWER BODY

It is extremely important *where* you sit in the saddle and how the lower trunk of the body fits into it. The saddle is not a chair. By and large, you want to sit in the middle of the saddle, not using the cantle as a backrest. The essential point is that in "sitting" on the saddle you actually ought to be sitting on the backs of your upper thighs and not on the buttocks. The joints that form the end of the thigh bone or femur are sometimes called the "sitting bones" and these are the basis for contact with the saddle. The buttocks themselves should be up and to the rear, placed softly against the face of the cantle. The beginner is often tempted to allow the buttocks to slip underneath him, causing him to round the back and shift around like a sack of grain in the saddle.

THE UPPER BODY

The lower back—the loins—are almost a third "aid" (along with hands and legs), as we shall see later. The small of the back, the area just above your belt, should be slightly hollowed out or made concave and then held with a mild degree of rigidity. The spinal column itself should be straight. You should sit erect, but without stiffness or tension, except for that moderate amount of tightening in the small of the back. A modest drawing back of the shoulders—but not a military brace—will help increase balance. The head is held up, and you should be looking forward to where you're going.

THE HANDS

The hand holding the reins should be a trifle above and in front of the horn, with the reins in very light contact. The elbows should fall naturally against the sides of the body. The "free" hand should never be stiffened or used awkwardly as some sort of "outrigger." Some beginners look as if they're trying to carry a pail of water in their opposite hand. Outside the show ring, it's not too important just where you place that empty hand, but resting it on the thigh makes sense. Don't get in the habit of resting it on the saddle horn.[3]

GENERAL IMPRESSIONS OF THE POSITION

The position I've been describing remains basic (with some small modifications) for the three natural gaits of the horse: the walk, the trot, and the gallop—or the walk, jog, and lope, in western parlance. It is not extremely difficult to arrange yourself in this position at the halt or at the walk, but it becomes trickier to keep this position as the horse moves into the jog and lope. For this reason it is necessary to spend enough time at the walk to make sure that this position is consistent, that you can hold it more or less unconsciously, before increasing the speed and motion of the horse.

You must get in your mind a pretty fair idea of the basic elements of this position, like a checklist, and then check on each part of the body to make sure that it is in the correct attitude. You do not have an instructor to holler, "Heels down!" or "Leg in!" so you have to be continually conscious of these fundamentals from the very first and develop the habit of constant self-criticism.

When you put together all these elements in combination, from the ball of the foot against the stirrup tread to the hand on the rein, what you have is a position in which the body of the rider is more or less in a straight line from the ankle joint to the hip joint to the back of the head. The appearance is the antithesis of a slouch, especially if you remember not to sit on your buttocks; you are erect, but without any artificial stiffness. Very little moves. It is a still position. Viewed from the side, your position gives the impression of balance and, therefore, security.

Introducing the Aids

The term "aids" refers principally to the effects created by the

---

[3]The horn appears to most beginners as a handy safety devide to be grabbed in case of loss of balance. It isn't. Gripping the horn tends to destroy what balance the rider has, even hastening his falling off. For this reason it's a poor practice, while learning, even to rest the hand on the horn or the swell fork.

use of the hands, the legs, and, secondarily, the voice.[4] I'm inclined to think that the lower back ought to qualify as an aid, too. At this stage of work, you will be concerned with the hand and leg aids, because you will want to stop and start and turn the horse to the left and right. It would be hard to avoid these fundamentals!

First, let's assume that you and your horse are at the halt. The objective is to move the horse forward. This provides you with the first opportunity to use the leg aids. The horse is moved forward by "closing" the legs, which means tightening the leg muscles against the horse's "barrel" or midsection where the cinch is located. On a reasonably well-trained horse, that is all that's required. The horse's barrel is round like a water glass, and you use the legs as you would tighten your fingers to get a firmer hold on a glass. The effect of this action of the legs is to urge the horse forward, to create "impulsion," and also to ask the horse to more fully engage the bit. But at this stage you are not concerned with pushing the horse onto the bit, so keep the hand relaxed and do not draw it back as the horse steps into the walk.

Normally, this closing of the legs to bring the horse from the halt to the walk is not very aggressive. You are not asking for sudden acceleration. The firmness of the leg aids will depend on the horse involved. But should the horse resist this more or less gentle squeezing, the leg muscles can be progressively tightened. Finally, if that doesn't get the job done, the heel can be brought into play, with a quick, light stroke delivered behind the cinch. A word of caution, though: always commence with the lightest possible leg aids. Don't use the heel unless absolutely necessary; otherwise your skill with the leg aids won't develop and you'll get into the habit of crudely "booting" horses around. This closing of the legs, by the way, ought not actually move the leg or change its position. From the bystander's vantage point, you should appear to be doing nothing.

You now have the horse walking forward. The leg aids can be further used, if necessary, to lengthen the stride at the walk, to encourage the horse to "walk out" in a bright, cadenced fashion.

---

[4]The voice can be decidedly useful in training, but talking to the horse (or, even worse, clucking to it) is not a good habit for the riding student. You are penalized in the show ring for voice cueing, too. "Talk" to the horse with your legs and hands.

The position at the free walk. The horse is relaxed, moving ahead with its head down and extended. The rider's position remains erect, but also without tension. The angle of this photo shows the rider sitting with the upper thighs only against the seat of the saddle.

The horse at the walk should, in general, be at its extreme speed at that gait most of the time. Don't allow the horse to stumble ahead in some slow, uneven, lethargic walk.

Now you must halt the horse, and this introduces the first use of the hand aids. There are three important general observations to be made about the hand aids in western equitation: (1) the western horse is not ridden on continuous contact with the mouth; (2) the hand aids are used primarily to cue or "signal" the horse rather than to restrain it; (3) the hand aids are almost never employed in a steady, continuous tightening of the rein, but, instead, the hand "pulls and releases" in a series of quick rein effects. It's a good idea to keep these principles in mind as I'll be referring to them often, both directly and indirectly.

To halt the horse from the walk is easy enough. You simply engage the bit momentarily by a quick squeezing of the rein with your fingers, the hand closing for an instant as if you were squeezing a rubber ball. This slight action is enough to activate the bit, causing the trained horse to stop. Remember that it's a quick squeeze or tightening of the fingers and an equally quick release, about as long as it takes you to count "one." If a single closing of the fingers on the rein doesn't completely halt the horse, repeat it again with equal briskness. If that does not succeed (although it should), exert a sharper rein effect by a slight backward cocking of the wrist as the fingers close. In most cases, any difficulties that arise are due to the rider's not being in contact with the horse's mouth and consequently squeezing on a totally slack rein so that no effect is produced in the horse's mouth.

Stop and start the horse several times. Decrease the time intervals between stopping and starting, so that after a while you can "turn on and off" like pushing buttons on a light switch.

All of this work has been done on the track. Now you'll want to be able to change the horse's direction. This objective introduces "reining" at the most elementary level. Reining is simple in principle, extremely complex in execution. The reins function as a *cue:* the horse turns in response to the rein against its opposite neck because it has been trained to do so.[5] There is no force or restraint involved. You are merely giving the horse a command, not physically forcing him to turn.

The first principle of reining is easy to state: the rider's hand points in the desired direction, the horse responds. It is deceptively easy. If you want the horse to turn to the left, the hand (holding the reins, of course) moves in that direction, as if pointing toward a target. The hand moving toward the left causes the rein on the opposite side to press against the horse's neck and the horse's forehand turns accordingly. Difficulties crop up, though, because of the beginner's tendency to do any one of three things: (1) raise the reining hand (often almost up to the chin); (2) pull the hand back, twisting the horse's head; or (3) swing the hand far out in the desired direction, far outside the line of the rider's body.

These common faults suggest some corresponding rules: (1) Don't raise or lower the reining hand; (2) Never pull the rein back; (3) Don't move the hand outside the line of the body. Keep the reining hand on the same level plane of the customary hand position. The horse turns on a loose inside rein, and you don't want to tighten the opposite or "bearing" rein because if you do

[5]Horses do not "neck-rein" naturally. Young horses are started by using a two-handed, direct reining technique in which the horse is compelled to turn by rein pressure. Later, the horse gets the idea that the neck rein is also a cue for a change of direction.

you'll pull against the bit on that side. In most instances, you can get the desired rein effect without bringing your hand outside the outline of the body.

The hand aids, if you think about it, control the portion of the horse in front of the cinch—or its "forehand." But the leg aids direct those parts of the horse behind the cinch—the "haunches." It stands to reason, then, that if you're going to turn the horse, the hand aids must be supported and supplemented by the leg aids. This is the first instance of an almost universal rule: *the aids are used in conjunction with one another,* they cooperate, they are in harmony, one sometimes is balanced against the other.

In the case of a simple turn, the cueing or reining hand is supported by an action of the leg *on the turning side.* A horse reined to the right, for example, is aided in making the turn by the rider closing or tightening the right leg against the horse. The horse then yields to this leg pressure, shaping his own body, to some extent, along the curve of the turn. This "inside" leg also stimulates the horse, creating more impulsion, not very necessary at the walk but vital for turns at the jog, lope, and fast gallop. The opposite leg is "passive;" it doesn't have to act unless the horse resists by swinging its haunches away from the curved line. If this happens, the otherwise passive leg also closes, preventing the "escape" of the haunches.

You are prepared, now, to turn the horse, using hand and leg aids in combination. In order to practice this movement efficiently, it is time to begin to learn to ride "school figures." School figures are patterns of movement or maneuver used in the ring not only to educate the rider, but also to further the education of the horse. They form the basis of training. Virtually all types of serious horsemanship employ school figures, although they are mostly associated in peoples' minds, I suppose, with dressage. These school figures are generally the same in all forms of equitation, but in stock-horse training some additional ones are used, such as figure-eight patterns and "doubling" figures. I will describe six of these school figures during various stages of development.

In order to get experience doing some simple reining at the walk, you can start with the two most fundamental of the school figures: the *Half-Turn* and the *Circle.* The Half-Turn is done like this: assuming you are on the track, make a half-circle toward the

51

center of the ring. To start with, this half-circle can be fairly large. As you complete the half-circle, angle the horse back toward the track on a straight, oblique line of about 45 degrees. When the forehand of the horse reaches the track, straighten the horse on the track and proceed ahead, in the opposite direction, of course, from the one you began with. In diagram form, the Half-Turn looks like this:

Half-Turn

The Circle figure can be made in various sizes. Start with circles of about thirty feet in diameter. To perform the Circle, turn your horse off the track toward the center of the ring and describe an even, really spheroid circle, returning to the track at the point where you left it, continuing on in the same original direction, as shown below:

Circle

These school figures appear simple, but they must be ridden with precision to get the full benefit from them; later, at gaits beyond the walk, you will find them a good deal more challenging. Not only should the figures be regular in shape, but the pace of the horse should be steady and as the figures progressively decrease in size, the "bending" of the horse on the curved lines becomes much more pronounced, requiring greater skill with the aids.

Working at the walk still, make the first attempts at these two figures rather large, concentrating on the harmonious cooperation of the hand and leg aids. Since you can now also halt the horse and move it forward, mix up stopping and starting with the figures. While all this is taking place, don't forget your mental checklist of the basic position. Be aware of how you're sitting. Check your heel and ankle position particularly—there is a temptation to draw up the heel on the turning side as you maneuver the horse, but this is very wrong. Make certain you haven't tucked the buttocks underneath and that you remain straight up in the saddle. Don't allow the lower legs to creep forward, look down at your knees and make sure only a small tip of the boot can be seen. Keep the hand relaxed and supple.

The contact you have with the horse's mouth is a delicate matter. Later, there will be times when you can work on a slack rein, but for now try to experiment with keeping an extremely light contact. Only experience will accustom your hand to this proper feel, but it is much better to be too light than too heavy. You must, though, learn the gradations of contact. Stop once in a while and slack the reins and then pick them up, adjusting your rein length by gradually making light contact. At the end of a learning session, by all means feed the horse a long rein, slack off and let your mount drop its head and walk on a free rein. Every time you ride a horse, incidentally, you should begin with about ten minutes at the walk, so as to warm up slowly, and then spend the last ten minutes of the ride walking down in a free, relaxed manner. As the horse is walking down, you can drop the stirrups, let the legs hang down, and allow the body to slouch, become limp and limber.

Horsemanship Dismounted

Horsemanship covers a wide range of skills. The complete horseman is a lot more than just a rider. There are literally hundreds of abilities you ought to acquire, as your education continues and many of them, even most of them, are only indirectly concerned with riding. For a person just beginning to ride, the more varied experiences he can have with horses the better. Some of these experiences are involved with practical necessities like saddling, but all are means by which you can develop those instincts that are so vital to a horseman.

At this stage of horsemanship, there are about four activities that are both valuable and appropriate for you to become familiar with: grooming; saddling; care of the horse in the barn (feeding, stall cleaning, etc.); longeing (if you have a horse "broke" for the longe line).

It is beyond the scope of this book to offer detailed, step-by-step instructions on grooming, saddling, and stable care, but there are many sources of information available on these subjects (see the appendix for some references).

Some western horses are taught to work on a *longe line* and some aren't. Most should. A longe line (or lunging line, as the British call it) is a long, flat web strap, usually about thirty-five feet in length, with a buckle or snap at one end and a loop or handhold at the other. It is attached to the horse's halter or, occasionally, to a bridle or, even better, to what is called a "longeing caveson." So rigged up, the horse is worked in a circle around the trainer (who holds the opposite end of the line, of course) in both directions and at all the gaits. It is an extremely important training and conditioning technique, but it is also a handy way to exercise or warm up a horse. Actually, longeing in serious training work is quite an art and requires knowledge and experience to use effectively. On the other hand, longeing a well-broke horse is an excellent way for a novice horseman to get experience in basic horsemastership. For this reason, it is worthwhile to spend a brief time discussing how to longe.

Besides the longe line and caveson, you will need a longe whip. The typical longe whip is six or seven feet long with a slightly longer lash that has a silk "popper" on the end. Don't longe without the whip. It is an essential part of any form of longeing, except perhaps just giving the horse a little casual exercise.

Lead the horse to the ring or corral and face him toward your left hand, with the line in that hand and the whip in the other. The longe line is always held in the hand toward which the horse is moving, assuming you are standing at right angles to the animal. The whip, in the opposite hand, is used essentially for controlling the horse's haunches. This arrangement means, of course, that when you change the horse's direction, you must switch the line and the whip into the appropriate hands. Standing at right angles to the horse, then, command, "Walk," and allow the horse to walk forward, circling around you in a small circle. You will increase the size of the circle as the horse works. Some fresh horses won't walk at first, so you may have it circling around you at the trot or even the gallop for a time. After about five minutes to the left, command, "Halt." Bring the horse toward you, move to his off side, his head facing to your right, and move him out again.

The whip should be held low, its tip aimed at the haunches. The trainer should always be parallel to the horse, line to the head, whip pointing toward the hindquarters. It may not be necessary actually to use the whip at all. It is primarily a signaling implement to prevent the haunches from swinging in or out and to urge the horse forward, if necessary. You do not normally hit the horse with the whip, but you may, on occasion, want to "pop" it if the animal gets lazy or if it doesn't respond to your voice commands to trot or gallop.

A good work on the longe line consists of about twenty or thirty minutes, with equal time to the left and right (except in unusual circumstances). Five minutes at a time in each direction is about proper. Walk the last ten minutes.

Don't try to longe a horse that is not already longe-trained. You will just get in a mess. But longeing is good experience for you if you have access to a horse that you can longe without difficulty. You can learn about individual horses by watching them on the longe line. It is also a first step toward learning about training—and riding and training are inseparable functions.

3

Finding the Balance

It shouldn't take a great deal of touring the ring at the walk before you can progress to trying the slow trot or jog. Perhaps, as a matter of fact, your horse has already taken a few steps at the trot while moving along the rail and you have felt that mild bouncing sensation that the trot produces. That sensation is created by the fact that at the trot the shoulders of the horse alternately rise and fall, where the shoulders are level at the walk and gallop. The trot is a two-beat gait in which a forefoot and the opposite hind hoof strike the ground simultaneously, followed by a similar "diagonal" with the other two feet. The head position is stationary.

Some beginning riders seem to have a sort of predispositon to dislike the trot because they believe they'll be unmercifully bounced up and down. That needn't happen. In the first place, there are ways of adjusting position to avoid being jumped up and down by the horse's shoulders and, in the second place, this potentially uncomfortable thrust is really only noticeable if the horse extends himself at the trot—and the western horse is rarely extended to this degree, working primarily at the slow trot or jog.

The trot is an important gait in western horsemanship. Many uninformed people think that western horses walk and lope but work very little at the trot. The trot is the principal trail gait; it becomes the best compromise between making time cross-country and conserving the horse's strength. The trot is the best means, perhaps the absolutely essential means, of conditioning the horse. Last, the trot is an exceptionally pleasant gait to ride, despite the beginner's initial doubts.

The western style of horsemanship is primarily concerned with the jog. This is a slow trot; in the show ring, in pleasure classes, you might call it the slowest trot. It is a true, two-beat trot, but the horse is not covering much ground. He is jogging ahead, slow, relaxed, not pushing much from the haunches and still on a loose rein. At this variation of the trot, the elevation of the shoulders is very slight and the motion created does not really jar the rider. It is perfectly comfortable to sit on the horse's back, absorbing the mild thrust of the jog.

First Attempts at the Jog

When attempting the jog for the first time, the main objective is to hold the position you've acquired at the walk—to remain in balance. While the center of gravity of the horse does shift forward at the jog, this forward progress is very minimal, so much so that there is no need to alter the position of the rider. When you try the jog, keep three simple aims in your mind: keep the heels down and the legs still; don't move your rein hand; slightly brace the small of your back. The heels must remain down so that the stirrups can carry weight; the legs must not move so that they remain under the body. By keeping your hand still, you won't be tempted to use the reins as a "handle," trying to get some false security by pulling the rein. By slightly stiffening your lower back, you'll stay erect and close to the horse's spine. That stiffening of the back, forcing your body against the horse's spine, will also encourage the horse to engage its hindquarters, which is desirable at the jog.

To put the horse on the jog from the walk, close the legs slightly and *gradually* squeeze the horse into the short trot. The horse should come on to the jog like thick syrup being poured out of a bottle. The transition from walk to jog should not be abrupt,

*The position at the jog. The rider's position displays maximum
balance, the rein hand relaxed and in mild contact with the mouth.
Notice the secure support provided by the leg position.*

and the jog itself should be *slow.*[1] As the horse moves into the
jog for the first few steps, common reactions among some
beginners are any of the following: sticking the feet out in
front, leaning backward, rounding the back, raising the hand,
or drawing up the heels. Resist these temptations by keeping in
mind how to respond to any feelings of loss of balance: step
even deeper into the stirrups, bring the leg in against the horse,
and stiffen the back some more.

Jog for only a short stretch at first, perhaps the long side of
the ring. You should attack the problem of learning the jog by
attempting relatively short bursts at first, trying to hold your
position only briefly. Close the fingers on the reins very much
as you did to effect the halt, and the horse will walk in
response. The last beat or two before the horse actually walks
will seem rougher, and it is at this point when you must
particularly concentrate on not letting your position collapse.

[1] In technical language, changes of gait and changes in variations of gait (like walk
to trot or slow gallop to ordinary gallop, etc.) are called *transitions.* It is common,
too, to speak of "upward" and "downward" transitions, meaning transitions
involving either lengthening or shortening stride or degrees of collection.

A common fault of a beginner at the jog. The legs have slipped, heels up, denying support; the back no longer acts as a shock-absorber. The insecurity of the seat leads to a paralysis of the hand. Contact lost, the horse is already "winging" ahead into a long trot.

Another common fault at the jog. Here, the student is leaning away, legs propped forward, trying to avoid the slight shock of the trot. The buttocks are under the body, and the hand is far out of position.

You're in, now, for a fairly lengthy period of repetition. You're going to just walk and jog and walk and jog on the track, gradually extending the periods at the jog, maintaining your position at the same time. Some things cannot be taught directly or verbally, and finding your balance at the jog is an instance of this. You simply must pound away at the trot for as long as necessary to the point where you can hold your position consistently. If you watch your leg position, sit deep, keep your hand free, and don't slouch above the hips, the breakthrough will come. You'll discover, sometimes almost in a flash, that sitting the jog is comfortable, effortless, and that you can relax and stay in balance with the horse.

Aids and Figures

When that happy occasion presents itself, you can direct your attention to the hand aids and, in extension, to approaching the few school figures at the jog. Your hand has really been inactive during this early "find-the-balance" stage, but it does have an important role to play at the jog. When you can sit in balance, then you can be concerned with what the horse is doing at the jog.

You have been moving on to the jog with the leg aids—very tactfully, because if you use too much leg stimulation, the horse will move ahead too boldly. But let's assume that that happens, that the horse goes from the walk to a brisk trot, perhaps even lengthening stride into a "buggy-horse" gait. Obviously you'll have to check him with your hand. In this instance, you'll close the hand and release in about the same manner you would employ if you were asking the horse to halt; a series of little, light squeezes will induce the horse to shorten stride. Suppose the opposite situation arises; the horse, while jogging, decides to slip back into the walk. This is prevented, of course, by use of your legs. In essence, your hand aids shorten the stride and your legs increase it. In order, then, to maintain evenness of pace at the jog—the first requirement of performance at this gait—there must be a balance, a harmony, between hand and leg. Since the jog is slow (the stride is short), a *light* contact with the mouth preserves this, but leg pressure contributes not only the necessary impulsion to stay on the jog, but also "pushes" the horse to the bit, the haunches active, maintaining not only a short but also a "cadenced" trot.

This is a delicate balance, and it is impossible, in technical terms, to tell you exactly how much hand and leg to use, except to repeat that the use of the aids should be quite light, the range of pressure not very great. You must develop the ability to react to the movement of the horse underneath you so that you can interpose the combination of hand and leg aids with the correct firmness and reciprocity. Remember that a good jog is slow, steady, and mildly springy. Remember, too, that the ability to use these aids, especially the hand, depends on the security of your seat, so you cannot slight the period of drill at the jog, getting yourself to the place where the general body position is consistent and in balance. It is easy to say this, but the process itself is far less so. The theory involved is relatively simple, but to arrive at this degree of security may take a while. Well-coordinated students can usually attain this goal in about two to three hours (in a lesson situation). This doesn't mean that you're polished at the jog, but that you do have sufficient balance to attempt school figures.

The first school figures to use are the ones you already know, the Half-Turn and the Circle. The first attempts at these figures usually present a problem. While the figure is completed, the horse has not jogged the whole figure; it has returned to the walk at some point. This has happened for one of two reasons: the balance of the rider has been inadequate, thus hampering the action of reining, or the rider hasn't been forceful enough with the inside leg, the leg on the turning side. Unless the rider is well balanced, the reining hand will be restricted, and there will be a tendency either to use the rein unevenly or to pull it back. The inside leg on a turn acts as an "accelerator pedal"; without its use, often vigorously, the horse will fall off gait as its stride shortens in small school figures or reining patterns. Be conscious of the need to use that inside leg to keep the horse "up" and moving.

If you can do the Half-Turn and the Circle figures reasonably well, smoothly, then you can try two more figures: the *Half-Turn in Reverse* and the *Serpentine*. The Half-Turn in Reverse is potentially confusing, but the diagram below will help. To do the Half-Turn in Reverse, leave the track at a forty-five degree angle toward the center of the ring. Proceed about fifteen to twenty feet (to start with) and then perform a half-circle back to the track. It is the Half-Turn with the two elements reversed in order. Straighten the horse up and go on along the track in the opposite direction. It looks like this:

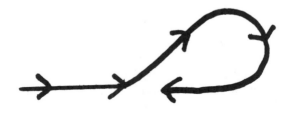

Half-Turn in Reverse

This is a trickier figure than the ones you've tried before. It requires briskness with the aids. Even more interesting is the Serpentine. This figure involves taking the horse off the track at about forty-five degrees (again, to start with), then bending him back toward the track at the same angle. When you reach the track, straighten the horse and then perform another "loop" and continue these loops along the whole side of the ring. In diagram, the figure is this:

Serpentine

The Serpentine calls for rapid alternations of the hand and leg aids, particularly when later you'll shorten up the distances involved.

Try both figures first at the walk for familiarization; then have a go at them at the jog. All of these figures will test your balance and the quickness and precision of your aids. At this stage, that balance will depend primarily on the lower half of the body (sometimes called the "base of support" in traditional riding manuals). That balance will arise from the supporting effect of the stirrups, plus the ability to come on to the horse's spine, so supported. The upper body (often called the "balance") is not only a necessary adjunct to balance, but its role in that balance will increase as you begin to maneuver at more speed. Riding the Serpentine, for example, you may notice that, as the horse performs very gentle swings, there is an impulse for the upper body to lean with the turn. That is a good impulse (about which we'll have more to say later). Occasionally, though, a student will want to lean *away* from the turns—which is usually the result of his being "behind" the horse, too far away from its center of gravity.

There are certain variations you can use for the Serpentine. In these variations it's very handy to have a set of six or more "poles," similar to those used in "pole-bending."[2] Set them in a row and serpentine through them. Don't get fancy too soon and ask the horse for sharp turns; set the poles, for the jog, at twelve to sixteen feet apart to start with. These poles can be set anywhere in the ring so that you can be working, now, away from the track. When you can perform the Serpentine at the jog through the stakes, try this augmented figure: ride through the stakes, do a half-circle around the last one, and then serpentine back. This is, in fact, a pole-bending pattern done at the jog with shortened distances between the stakes.[3] This pattern is demand-

---

[2] These poles or stakes can be made simply. An easy way is to take eight-foot doweling sections, one or two inches in diameter, and cement them into two-pound coffee cans. You can also use oil drums ("barrels"), but I much prefer the poles. Or you can use those plastic, cone-shaped highway markers, if you can get them. As you will see later, there are quite a number of uses for a set of these poles.
[3] The conventional distance between the poles for pole-bending at the fast gallop is twenty-one feet. That distance is specified by the American Quarter Horse Association. Remember that these early Serpentine exercises are *not* pole-bending games, but instructional techniques.

ing because of the short half-circle at the end of the row. Your horse is apt to subside into a walk unless you are vigorous with the inside leg. You will notice that there's a rhythm to the serpentine when it's done right. The jog should have an even cadence, and when this occurs the aids are applied in an almost rhythmical sequence as you work your way through the poles. The principal merit in this pattern is that its rapidity provides you with an opportunity to begin to use your aids instinctively—there isn't time for very much deliberation. But in this quickness, *don't* begin to jerk your hand or thrash around in the saddle. Keep cool. You can easily tell by how your horse works whether your aids are tactful, yet effective. The horse should move promptly and with an even flexibility.

You can now combine all these school figures in random sequences, interspersed with walk-jog transitions, upward and downward, with an occasional halt off the walk thrown in. Assuming that this can be done handily, you can now move to a much more difficult figure, the *Figure Eight.*

Riding the Figure Eight

This is a figure that is best done, at first, by taking it in parts. Consequently, you can approach it by first doing what is called the "Change of Hand" or "Change of Rein" (itself a basic school figure but of greater use in English horsemanship). You "change hands" by moving your horse out of the corner of the ring and crossing diagonally to the corner on the opposite side at the far end, and then continuing in the opposite direction. You can see in the diagram opposite that it is "half" of a figure-eight.

The figure eight itself is a much shortened pair of "changes of hand." Begin by riding a few changes of hand at the jog using the entire ring, linking together two such changes of hand so that you have ridden a figure eight incorporating the full ring area. The pattern seems simple enough. But now lay out two of your poles about twenty to thirty feet apart. They will mark the centers of the loops of your smaller Figure Eight. With these in place, you can ride your first compact version of the figure. Walk the pattern first, so that you can plan in your mind just how the aids will be used.

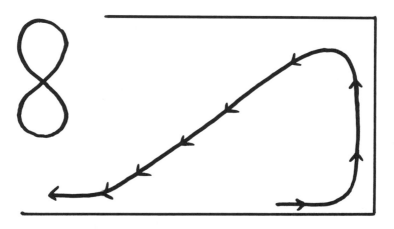

Change of Hand; Figure-Eight (inset)

In a way, the Serpentine was a transitional figure, because the figures that preceded it did not require that you "push" the horse much beyond some firmness with the inside leg. The Serpentine, on the other hand, demanded that you "ride" the horse a bit: you were asking the horse to perform a good deal beyond its routine inclinations, you were far more directing its movements. This meant, actually, that you were increasing the forcefulness of the leg aids *without* becoming aggressive with the hand. As you perform more difficult figures—like the Figure Eight—you will notice how the emphasis remains on the leg aids. The Figure Eight cannot be done at the jog without direction from the leg aids (as with the Serpentine), but it may also require you to use the leg to get some impulsion, some quick acceleration, if the horse seems to "die" on the short loops. You must be "leg conscious" when you take on the Figure Eight, and be prepared to use the heel as a part of the leg aids.

Use of the heel, when used, is delivered in a quick, light stroke behind the cinch or in a series of light strokes very much like a flutter. The heels are almost never used on both sides of the horse simultaneously. The advantage of the spur, by the way, is that it permits you to get a heel effect by only turning in the heel instead of drawing it back and out of position. The spur, correctly used, is simply a metal extension of the heel. If the heel is really a sort of

65

emergency form of the leg aid—used when the closing or tightening leg is not enough—then it must be employed with a great deal of quickness to be effective, or else the need for the augmented leg aid has already passed.

The Figure Eight should not, by now, present any unusual difficulties in reining. Keep the hand low with mouth contact light, wrist limp. Do not draw the hand back on the turns. Don't extend the reining hand outside the line of the body as a general rule. Regardless of what may happen, try hard to keep the rein pressure even.

Starting the Figure Eight, try to keep the two loops even and circular. Don't try to hug the pole markers at first; the main objective during the first trial runs at the Figure Eight is to smoothly jog the whole figure. This entails using the inside leg as the horse turns on the loops of the pattern. This leg action must be coordinated with the reining hand, which does not pull the horse around but only cues the forehand. If you desire to keep the horse on the jog throughout the figure, don't extend at the trot. Keep the same slow, cadenced pace.

It is a sound idea to do two Figure Eights at a time, but don't keep the horse working continually at this pattern. The horse's enthusiasm will wane by too much repetition. Vary work with the Figure Eight with other figures and with periods at the relaxed walk.

A lot will happen with this new emphasis on mobility. The horse is beginning to function, when you consider what you're asking him to do now in these school figures and all the combinations that they provide. This increasing preoccupation with performance—getting the horse through these patterns—will tend to divert your mind from attention to your own position, the harmony of your seat on the horse. There is a risk of becoming sloppy, letting legs and arms flap around or the body sway or slouch. Care must be taken to preserve the balance you've gained through a consistent position. This will demand that you concentrate on two things at once—performance and position. But the two are intimately related, and performance will be impaired unless you are checklisting position as you go.

Introducing the "Dwell"

Getting familiar with moving the horse through the school figures at the jog is accomplishing two things: developing balance, and sharpening the cooperation of the aids. Now you can begin to entertain methods of using the aids in a more complex way. This greater skill with the aids can start with a consideration of what is commonly called the "dwell."

To begin with, what you'll be concerned with is the *preliminary* use of the leg aids to prepare for the hand or rein cues. The term "dwell" refers to the instant at which the horse, prepared by the legs, is balanced and receptive to quick, assertive cues from the hand. The dwell will be used in a number of ways later, but now you will only become accustomed to the *habit* of closing the leg slightly *prior* to any request to the horse to make a quick response.

Let's deal with this on a more concrete, applied level. You can begin with the process of halting, or the "stop." So far you have been stopping from the walk by a quick engagement of the bit only. But what is really desired is to stop the horse "in one piece," to make a halt in which the horse commences to halt with the *hindquarters* first. To make this kind of a stop, you must cue the horse. This is done by closing the leg a *fraction of a second* before the hand aid is used. The effect of this technique on the horse is twofold: it pushes the horse on to the bit (making the hand action more effective) and it also "tells" the horse that some rapid response is impending. The horse is likely, therefore, to engage the haunches and begin the stop from the rear.

This first simple use of the dwell technique should be tried at the walk to begin with. It should be emphasized that the time lapse between the action of the leg and hand is only a split second. The beginner, at first, is apt to be far too slow. The use of the leg and hand are so close together as to virtually constitute only one act.

You won't notice much change in how the horse responds when you're practicing this at the walk. But you will see quite a change at the jog. In order to make a stop off the jog, there are some additional ingredients to be incorporated. The first is the action of the hand, and the second is the use of the back.

In stopping off the jog, the hand must not only close on the reins, but the wrist must be cocked back to the rear very rapidly, positively bringing the bit into play. The action of the hand is much like that of a tight spring: the hand suddenly draws back (either by the backward arc of the wrist or by a slight motion of the hand itself in toward the body) and is instantly released. The hand, in short, must be exceedingly quick. The more abrupt the stop, the more quickly the hand must be used.

A split second before the hand aid is employed, at the time when the legs commence the dwell, the rider's lower back must be tightened. There should be a noticeable stiffening, even a bracing of the small of the back. This must be done to encourage the engagement of the horse's haunches and to prepare the rider himself for the shock of the stop.

If you prepare the horse for the stop, you must prepare yourself. If the aids work, the horse is going to stop—and more abruptly than you might anticipate. In preparing for the stop, the important consideration is to keep your deep seat in the saddle; the jolt of the stop will tend to "prop" you forward, and you may lose contact with the saddle. To counteract this, while making sure that your legs are well engaged, concentrate on the brace with the small of the back, tightening the loin muscles. This action with the back will have the effect of keeping your sitting bones against the spine of the horse and driving your lower body downward and slightly forward. Do not lean backward. The two major faults of position to be avoided during the stop are propping forward and leaning to the rear. Remember, too, that there are no "brakes" on a horse. So it doesn't make any sense to push your lower legs forward during the stop. The brace provided by the stirrups is *downward,* not forward over the shoulders; keep your legs underneath you for balance.

In trying a modest stop off the jog for the first few times, I'd suggest that you "talk" to yourself: say to yourself, "Halt" (even out loud), and then, "One," applying the aids in sequence on this last count. The purpose of this is to get you into the habit of timing the stop—using the aids with speed and precision. Put the horse on the jog and try to stop. At first you're likely to be disappointed in your stop. The horse will not stop briskly; it will seem to halt in sections. This results from a lack of quickness with the hand and leg aids and a lack of coordination between the two. Even when stopping off the jog, the hand must act more swiftly than you estimate, the first time or two. You will get the hang of it after a few attempts; you can gauge your progress by the fact that when the horse stops properly, abruptly, "sticking his tail in the ground," you will be pushed slightly from the rear as the haunches engage first, while the spinal column (on which you're sitting) will be straight and relaxed.

Take two of your poles or stakes and set them like two gate posts on the track. This will provide you with a target, so that you can practice stopping on an imaginary line drawn between them. Don't sour the horse, by the way, by working on the stop for long periods. Intersperse work on the school figures at a walk and a jog so that you won't cause the horse to become fractious.

Backing

Asking the horse to back also calls into play that preliminary, preparatory action of the legs. From the halt, apply the legs lightly and then begin to slowly pulsate the tension on the reins by a series of squeezes. Do not pull hard on the reins and try to force the horse to back. Again, you are asking and not forcing, and the horse should respond by a slight lowering of its head and a backward step with one of the forelegs. Use the hand slowly at first so that the horse also backs slowly. The legs should continue to exert some pressure, preferably by tightening and then relaxing the calf muscles. It is very desirable for the horse to back straight, and the legs should be used to attempt to keep the rear quarters straight. Only back three or four steps at a time, then walk the horse forward, halt, and try again. Do not ask the horse to back more than a half-dozen times at the most during one session. Backing is quite tiring for a horse and should not be overdone. Also, for the present, back slowly; more speed can be introduced later. If the horse throws up his head and shows signs of resistance, don t fight back. Work the animal forward for a while. The resistance may be the result of too much pressure on the bit.

With increasing balance, it has been possible to use more complicated effects with the aids. Consistent balance provides the freedom of action that the advanced rein effects require. Secure at the jog—it should be as easy as sitting on a kitchen stool—the problem is to hone the aids to a fine edge and to move on to more demanding tests of your balance, as with the lope or slow gallop, acquiring as much smoothness at this gait as you have gained at the jog. The ability to work the horse at will on the school figures will also develop confidence. This confidence is more than just familiarity; it grows from your ability to consign certain features of your position in the saddle and certain aspects of your use of the aids to your subconscious mind. These techniques, then, are beginning to be instinctive; your nervous system is handling the responses rather than your thought processes. This is the beginning of real horsemanship.

4

The Final Gait

The gallop is the "final gait." The horse having three natural gaits, the gallop is the last one you'll need to encounter.[1] In western circles the slow gallop is termed the *lope*. The gallop comes in a number of variations, from the slow lope to the racing gallop, but the pattern of the gait, the way the horse puts his feet on the ground, is identical. Differences in these variations of the gallop are principally concerned with the length of stride. The gallop is a three-beat gait: the horse commences the gallop with a hind foot, followed by the opposite front foot, and then followed by a diagonal of the remaining front and rear feet. The galloping horse appears to roll along, his head describing a gentle arcing motion.

The western horse works primarily at the lope, although frequently he may be asked to increase speed (lengthen stride) virtually to his maximum capacity. The lope, though, is slow and,

---

[1] There are artificial gaits. Most of these are four-beat gaits, such as the "slow gait," and "rack" of the American Saddlebred, and other similar gaits, such as the "running walk," the "fox trot," and the "amble." Some Standardbreds also "pace" (a two-beat gait). Although some horses show a predisposition for these "auxiliary" gaits, they are not natural to the horse as a species (except for the pace in certain breeds).

like the jog, the slower the better, as a rule. It is also an economical movement, the hoofs moving close to the ground without much elevation of the knees.

Unlike the walk and the jog, the horse at the lope or gallop performs with his shoulders at an angle—or, more properly, with the point of one shoulder kept farther forward than the other. If you look down from the saddle at the shoulders of your horse at the walk or jog, you will see that the points of the shoulder are even, as below:

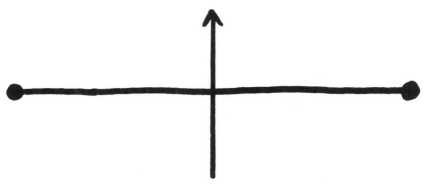

Position of the points of the shoulder at walk and trot

When the horse gallops, however, one of the shoulders will be kept in advance of the other, as shown:

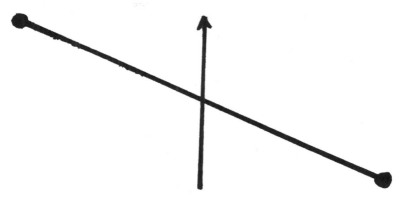

Position of the points of the shoulder at the gallop, left lead

This means, in fact, that one forefoot of the horse is consistently ahead of the other at the appropriate cycle of the gallop. You could say that the horse had a "leading" foot. In the terminology of equitation, this is spoken of as the "lead," so that at the gallop or lope the horse is traveling on either the right or the left "lead." This is not just equine trivia; this has a functional importance. If the horse is traveling on a straight line, it makes no particular difference which lead the horse is on as far as his balance and movement are concerned. But if the horse turns or circles to the left or right, the matter of leads becomes extremely pertinent, because the horse's balance is critically affected by the choice of lead. If turned to the left at the gallop, the horse is balanced *if* he is on the left lead, the left forefoot leading. Should he turn to the left with the right forefoot leading, he will manage to turn awkwardly because he is balanced *away* from the direction in which he is turning. If the turn is not too sharp, he'll probably negotiate it on the "wrong" lead (often called "false" or "counter" galloping), but the horse is sufficiently off balance on the wrong lead so that on a small or sudden turn he might fall.

Of course the stock horse, either working cattle or running reining patterns, must make very quick changes in direction. Obviously, these involve changes of lead, too. In short, the trained stock horse must be able to make very rapid lead changes as he works. This can be accomplished, by the way, because most horses have an inclination to gallop on the correct lead, although it is by no means certain he will do so. In any case, without prolonged training the horse cannot make these changes "on the fly." The untrained horse doesn't have the suppleness, in the first place, to make swift lead changes and a "green" horse must, in order to make a change of lead, come back to the jog or trot before switching. A primary necessity of stock-horse training is to teach the horse to change leads smoothly, quickly, and accurately.

Any movement in a riding ring is to the left or to the right, so the matter of leads comes up immediately when the lope is introduced. Working the ring to the left at the lope means having the horse on the left lead, and vice versa. The question of leads, then, complicates learning the lope, because, now, we have to consider not only the "transition" to the lope (from the walk or jog) but also the selection of the correct lead. Happily, as you'll

73

see shortly, the proper use of the aids can accomplish both objectives simultaneously.

Position at the Lope

What about the position at the lope? The problem with the position at the lope is not getting into it, but holding it. This problem is due, in part, to the beginner's attitude toward the lope itself. Learning to ride the lope represents a kind of psychological plateau. The beginner wants very much to do it—he usually has the idea that the lope is *the* gait of the western horse—but, at the same time, the lope seems much more energetic, even hazardous, than the jog. Many beginners have balance problems at first in the lope, usually as a result of the tendency to stiffen the body, partly, I think, because of some anxiety about keeping in balance. It is for this reason that it's not advisable to attempt the lope until the rider has really become comfortable and confident at the jog. With learning to ride (and with training horses, too), what seems the slow, methodical way is, in the end, the speediest.

There is no basic change of position for the slow lope. The center of gravity isn't forward enough yet to require any substantial change. The problem is to accustom yourself to holding your position while the horse is moving in an as yet unfamiliar way. The leg position remains the same, the lower body is deep into the saddle, and the upper body is erect without stiffness. This is easier said than done. At first, the motion of the gallop will tend to dislodge you.

For this reason, the first attempts at the lope must emphasize the transition to the lope, plus *short* distances at this gait—say the length of one long side of the ring. It is important to move with the horse as the transition is made from the jog and then to hold position for a short stretch. Most beginners display a variation of one of three basic faults during their first efforts at the lope:

They lean away from the impulsion of the horse, legs going forward, buttocks against the cantle. Usually this awkward position is accompanied by an elevation of the hand, sometimes almost to the chin. Often the elbows go out like chicken wings.

This inelegant, unbalanced position results from a spontaneous recoil from the thrust of the horse. The motion of the lope being

The position at the lope. The "basic position" is maintained. Notice that the rider appears to be sitting in the "middle" of the horse. The hand is independent and soft, using a somewhat longer rein than is customary in "equitation" classes in the show ring.

The beginner's most common fault at the lope. The student is trying to sit away from the horse's impulsion. Here the rider's legs do not support, and no balance is attained. A sudden move of the horse's haunches would dislodge the student, who is trying to balance himself with the reins.

unfamiliar and in some cases mildly intimidating, the rider unconsciously wants to avoid it, trying to lean away from it. Of course, he is behind the center of gravity, the legs no longer serving as a base of support, and the loss of balance that follows causes the rider to begin to sway, a somewhat alarming feeling that he frequently responds to by pushing his feet even farther forward and trying to brace himself against the cantle.

If this happens to you, rein up gently and put your position back together at the walk. You can correct this major fault by being "leg conscious," not permitting the legs to come forward towards the horse's shoulders as he begins to lope, and by keeping the body erect, not allowing the buttocks to slip underneath you. Try the lope again, nice and slow, along the long side of the ring. Bring your weight into the stirrups, hold your hand still, and slightly stiffen your back.

The second time should be better. The horse will feel "flatter" to you. This is because you're concentrating on keeping your legs under your body. You can find the balance at the lope as you did at the jog.

Another common response of the beginner to his first effort at the lope is to allow the heels to come up and the toes to go down, with the lower leg canted to the rear. The upper body then folds like an accordian, head down, shoulders rounded, back hunched. The insecurity of this position will cause the buttocks to bang the back of the saddle unpleasantly, the rider reacting by bending over even more, monkey-style.

Again, the leg position does not hold. There is no base of support; the rider is being jostled like a sack of grain and he may snatch the reins, trying to use them as a handle. Equally bad, he may latch on to the saddlehorn.

If this is your reaction, more or less, try again, riveting your attention on what your legs are doing and bowing in the small of your back. Don't tighten the rein; keep the rein hand limp. Square the shoulders. The keystone of the position is the heels, the bent ankle, to permit weight in the stirrups. Step hard on the stirrup tread, keeping the heels low. You'll be tempted to go on to your knees, that is, letting the lower leg slip and relying on the knee grip. Relax the knees, don't press them.

A reaction more difficult to correct can be described as a disinclination on the part of the rider to come on to, to sit against,

Another fault at the lope. The student has lost contact with the horse's spinal column; he's standing in the stirrups, knees tense. A lack of balance will lead to both insecurity and an inability to use either the hand aids or leg aids.

the horse's spine. In appearance, this fault gives the impression that the rider believes he would get an electric shock if he sat down. Technically, of course, the accomplished rider is *not* fully seated, as a considerable part of his weight is in the stirrups and he is surely not just plumping down his weight on the horse's spine. But the rider must sit *against* the spine, the seat of the saddle, giving the appearance that he's sitting deeply in the saddle. Some beginners resist coming down into the saddle, avoiding contact in a number of ways, the most common of which is a tendency to want to stand in the stirrups, the upper thighs hovering just above the seat of the saddle.

In some cases, this position, seriously wrong as it may be, does not *look* too out of whack; the leg position may appear reasonably correct and the body may be approximately upright in the saddle. In more extreme cases, though, the rider's position may look like the "forward seat"—as if the rider were in position to jump a five-foot fence—with his base of support in fair position but his upper body bent so far forward from the hip joints that the upper thighs have lost contact with the saddle. But even if the rider looks halfway correct, the fact is that he's avoided contact with the spine, even if only by a slim margin. And he's managing to do this by *stiffening the knee,* slightly changing the angulation of the leg position.

This disinclination to sit down, in blunt terms, arises from an anxiety about real contact with the horse at the lope. The best way to deal with it is to get over this anxiety by allowing the body to relax and accept the motion of the gallop. The place to start relaxing, if you have this tendency, is in the knees. Don't tense the knees; hold them only tight enough to prevent slippage, and then let the lower torso ease down into the comfort of the saddle, buttocks gently against the cantle. If you do this, you will get an immediate feeling of increased balance, which will further encourage you to relax and "sit loose," not sloppily or without leg support, but without excessive rigidity. Actually, the horse's backbone is a good place to be at the gallop, provided, of course, that the horse has not extended the gallop to the point where his center of gravity is so far forward that you must bring your weight correspondingly forward, closer to the withers. Sometimes it is not this simple to correct the fault under discussion, as if the student had some built-in aversion to sitting down. In difficult cases, it is helpful to try the slow lope without the use of stirrups for a time, forcing the rider to come deeper into the saddle as he has no stirrups to stand in. But this should be only a temporary expedient, and, on balance, riding without stirrups at the gallop introduces more problems than it solves.[2]

In all these instances, the problem is to accept the motion of the lope or gallop. Even if you don't have these difficulties to face or only have a mild case, so to speak, this accommodation to the movement of the lope takes a certain amount of time to effect.

---

[2]Contrary to popular opinion, a great deal of bareback riding or riding without stirrups is *not* beneficial to developing a sound position and, still less, tactful aids. Without the stirrups, the best of riders cannot have complete freedom of the hand; bad habits, like allowing the buttocks to slip underneath the body, follow from too much riding without stirrups. The benefits of riding without stirrups or bareback are really only two: sometimes confidence is gained, and it is a fine way to tighten flabby leg muscles quickly. But these benefits do not outweigh the liabilities.

This is one stage in your equestrian education in which an instructor, even if you had one, is only useful for reminding you of the theoretical principles involved. You must, by yourself, really learn how to sit at the lope and this is done primarily by slowly extending the distance at which you can lope in balance and confidence. What you must avoid are serious losses of balance. Remember that you're training your nervous system as well as your conscious mind. Don't try to "hang on" at the lope when you feel you have a substantial loss of balance. Pull up, in that case, to the walk, recover your position, and start again.

Putting the Horse on the Lope

The first efforts at making the transition to the lope should be done from the jog. That's because it's easier; we'll consider going to the lope from the walk a bit later. What is involved is a *cue*, a precise signal to the horse that at once asks for the lope and indicates the desired lead. This cue goes as follows: let's suppose you want to move from the jog into the lope while tracking left in the ring, calling, then, for a left lead. First, prepare the horse to lope by being certain you have his attention—by a very slight tightening of the leg or a little squeeze with the fingers. The cue itself is given with a *simultaneous* action of hand and leg. Squeeze the *right* leg firmly and briskly. You will notice that the action of the leg is always on the side of the horse *opposite* from the leading side or, put another way, the intended direction.[3] This sudden leg pressure will encourage the right hind leg of the horse to commence the cycle of the gallop, following, in the next beat, with the extension of the left foreleg. At the *exact* instant this leg is engaged (the other leg entirely passive), the hand is moved slightly to the right (just off the line of the horse's crest) and momentarily the reins are squeezed and the hand drawn back. The hand then releases with equal briskness. The rein effect will encourage the opening of the shoulder to the left in conjunction

[3] This is not the only "cue" for what classical riding terms the "gallop depart." The method suggested above is a variation of what is often called a "gallop depart on the outside lateral aids." Highly collected horses can be galloped off the "inside lateral aids," the cues on the side to which the horse's forefoot will be leading. There are also the so-called "diagonal aids," not of much pertinence to western horsemanship.

with the action of the leg. It is extremely important that the leg and hand aids occur together, simultaneously. This cue is *not* the "dwell effect" discussed earlier.

As the horse instantly responds to this cue (as it will *if* the aids are used together), close both legs with a moderate firmness so as to confirm, as it were, the action of the lope. For a right lead, of course, the opposite aids are used.

Don't be disappointed that the horse doesn't respond with quite the precision you'd like the first time or two. It takes a while to coordinate the parallel action of hand and leg aids. That lack of coordination is the most common reason for difficulties in the beginning. Also, at times students are apt to be too vigorous with the hand, drawing it back too far or too aggressively and not releasing it quickly enough. On the well-trained horse, the cue for the lope is quick and authoritative, but it is also subtle. You don't need to pound and jerk. In fact, properly done, the action of the leg is invisible to the bystander and the action of the hand is very limited. Often a mere squeeze on the rein, combined with a cue from the outside leg, is entirely sufficient to ask for a lope.

Never attempt to put the horse on the lope by merely driving it on into an extended trot and then breaking over, awkwardly, into a gallop. If you miss the cue for the lope, come back to the slow jog and try again in a calm and collected manner. This transition should be smooth, effortless, deliberate, and quiet; the horse should not burst into the lope. If that happens, your aids have been too forceful. The cue for the lope is an ideal example of the most elementary principle of using the aids on the western horse: the aids are a form of communication—they *ask* the horse—and they do not force. Therefore, incidentally, don't expect to do transitions into the lope like this on an untrained horse. He won't know what you're asking for.[4]

Many horses develop a distinct reaction to voice commands. Veteran show horses will even be inclined to pick up orders to move on from the ring announcer's directions. Strings of school horses I've worked through the years invariably pick up my voice

[4] Green horses are taken to the lope in early stages of training by direct, forceful means of positioning them and utilizing their raw impulsion. But this is a necessity of training and not a principle of equitation. Even in training, longe work greatly aids in teaching the young horse how to lope properly so that voice commands can reduce the aggressiveness needed by legs and hands, but only in training situations.

commands and respond to them. Young horses in training are often worked with voice commands. But, strictly speaking, the voice is not a genuine aid in more sophisticated forms of horsemanship. This being true, don't start out by clucking or vocally urging on your horse while making the transition to the lope. Talking to your horse may be sociable while working him, but don't let it become an unconscious habit. Voice cueing is frowned upon in the show ring. Leave the exhorting to the Lone Ranger, and speak to your horse with the conventional aids of leg and hand.

Getting the Feel of the Lope

Working the track at the slow lope is the inevitable way of coming to feel really comfortable at this gait. Once that feeling of comfort and security comes over you—and it may happen with relative suddenness—the pleasure is very considerable. Most people prefer the slow lope to all other gaits. The slow lope has a gentle rocking motion; the shoulders of the horse do not rise (as they do at the jog) and as the horse increases speed at the gallop he will feel even "flatter." In a manner of speaking, the two easiest gaits to sit are the walk and the flat-out run. This feeling of comfort comes from balance, of course, and that balance results from the consistency of your position. But beyond the necessary concentration on your body position, you must also be aware of what your hands are doing. Your newly found balance will be displayed by what you can now do with your free hand (the one that's not holding the reins). Likely, when you started out at the lope, that hand acted like a sort of stiff rudder, held out from the body. Some students look as if they're trying to carry an invisible bucket of water. But now notice that you can let that hand fall relaxed at your side, or carry it without stress on your thigh. You can even reach up and pull down your hat or rub your nose. Make use of this new freedom; accentuate the balance of your overall position by doing some simple exercises with your free hand and arm. Wave your arm around in circles, hold it out straight from your shoulder, and as you approach the corner of the ring, point at some spot on the ring surface and keep pointing at it as your horse lopes around the end of the arena. There's a curious thing

81

about learning the lope (once you've learned how to ride it in balance): it helps the learning process if you work at something that distracts you from direct attention to how you're sitting, focusing your interest on what the horse is doing instead of on what you're doing. The next chapter is largely made up of work of this type. You are beginning, then, to ride "instinctively" instead of deliberately.

The rein hand deserves attention, too. Because of your temporary insecurity during your first attempts at the lope, it's a good bet that your rein hand moved around a good deal. Without essential balance, there's no freedom of the hand, as I've said before. You may have been tempted to balance with the rein, but even if you didn't, it's likely that your fingers and wrists grew a bit tense. It is also very possible that during this phase your contact with your horse's mouth was erratic; you lost contact altogether at times and you tightened up excessively at others. Now you must hold the reins so as to have a feather-light feel of the mouth at all times, a feel just short of loss of contact. Keep the hand still. This basic contact, established now at the slow lope on the rail, must, in future, be preserved when you maneuver the horse. Like feeling the lope itself, you will develop a feel for the smooth, delicate contact with the mouth, regardless of what movements the horse may undertake at the gallop.

Maneuvering at the Lope

At this point, you should be able to do two things consistently: Put the horse into the lope from the jog on the correct lead, and work the horse at the lope on the rail as many times around the ring as you choose with a good firm position. Beyond these accomplishments, we will want to be able to put the horse on the lope from the walk and begin to perform simple maneuvers at the slow lope.

There is no basic difference in the "gallop depart" from the jog or the walk insofar as the cueing is concerned. A greater degree of precision is called for if you do it from the walk, however. The exactness of leg and hand cooperation is vital; keep the leg aid, particularly, crisp and affirmative. You can master the knack of moving from walk to lope in two or three tries, as a rule; it is a matter of "inner tim ng." Sometimes a phlegmatic horse needs a touch of the spur at this point, if it's been a while since he's been asked to lope from the walk.[5]

You need not be too ambitious about learning to rein the horse at the lope. Take it in easy stages, beginning with a very large circle figure executed at either end of the ring. Pick up the lope along one long side of the arena, go into the corner, and describe a large circle figure. This simple figure will demonstrate the need to make the reining motion a flowing, continuous gesture with the hand. Keep the hand low and don't draw it back. If you have forgotten to rely on the inside leg as a means of flexing the horse and keeping his impulsion activated, as you learned in the earlier school figures, you may be surprised that the horse breaks into an uncomfortable trot somewhere on the circle. If so, don't forget the reinforcing leg the second time.

These circles are not hard to ride, so you can shortly begin to cut some circles off the rail at various places in the ring. Keep the circles no smaller than about thirty feet in diameter. The emphasis is on evenness of pace and regular curvature of the figure. As you practice these figures (and tighter ones later on), you should begin to pay attention to the use of the "outside" leg, the leg *away* from the turning side. In large figures, like these circles, the primary mission of the outside leg is to prevent the horse's haunches from swinging away from the curving line of the figure. As the figures become smaller, the inclination of the horse to avoid flexing the back by merely displacing the haunches off the line increases. Even if he doesn't offer this minor resistance, the sheer tightness of the figure will cause those haunches to drift. Your outside leg, then, becomes less passive; it is in more use as you bend the horse around in these smaller, tighter movements. However, this outside leg aid never is applied with as consistent vigor as the inside or turning leg aid, nor does it initiate a cueing.

These early circle figures, straightforward enough to ride as

[5] It is at this stage of instruction, by the way, that I usually allow and encourage the student to put on a pair of spurs. The orthodox, blunt-roweled spur is, in my opinion, a regular and necessary part of the rider's gear. It is an extension of the rider's heel and renders it possible to give the leg cues with much less force. You can make a ceremony of putting on the spurs, if you like, as their installation on the boot has been for centuries a ritual, a "rite of passage."

they may be, are nonetheless a test of the harmony of the hand and leg aids. They require, as the figures grow smaller, a more intimate, ongoing balance between the two.

Success at the circles bring you to the Change of Hand as the next figure to be loped. At the lope, this figure is far more complicated than it was at the jog. The change of direction involved, at the jog, was simple, but at the lope this change of direction requires a change of lead. Take care with this Change of Hand figure, because it's trickier than you think. Ride it the following way (using the full area of the ring):

Pick up the lope on the long side of the arena, in either direction, then continue around the end of the ring into the opposite corner; now cut diagonally across the ring to the far corner on the opposite side. You will see, as you emerge from the first corner and are crossing the ring diagonally, that you'll very soon be shifting direction—so that it will be necessary to make a change of lead. That change will be made as you pass the center of the ring. For the first few times while trying this figure, you can make that change by coming down to the jog as your horse crosses the dead center of the ring, allowing him to perform two or three beats or "diagonals" at the jog, then applying the appropriate aids to move back on to the lope on the new lead and then loping on into the far corner on this correct lead.

Try the Change of Hand in both directions, tracking left and right at the start. It is not a difficult movement once you have gotten used to making the downward transition and changing leads in the center of the ring. If you miss a lead change, come back to the jog and start again. That is a firm rule for all missed leads, incidentally. Of course, a good stock horse can make quicker changes of lead than this, which you can try when you reduce the size of the figure. Remember that two consecutive or linked changes of hand produce a Figure Eight (the figure that, finally, will concern you most).

While the Change of Hand figure is not all that demanding, it is necessary to try to ride it very evenly, and to time the lead change properly so that you perform it as close to dead center of the ring as you can manage. Your horse may have a tendency to hurry a little coming off the rail as you cross the arena. Keep the beats of the lope slow and even.

Do not just practice at the lope. Now that you can ride all three

84

gaits and have gotten skillful at the use of the basic figures (Half-Turns, Circles, Half-Turns in Reverse, Serpentines, and Changes of Hand) you have a whole repertoire to work with. Put it all together in as many combinations as you can think of. Use gait transitions and school figures together (remembering, of course, that, so far, you are doing only two of these figures at the lope: circles and changes of hand). Keep everything slow and rhythmical.

Moving On

With practice, you have become fully accustomed to the slow lope. Done properly, it's like selecting the gear on a car, but the gallop (which is, you will recall, the more technical or formal term for that three-beat gait of which the lope is a variation) comes in other forms. Western riding requires that we move on from time to time, going from the slow lope to a faster pace at the gallop. In some western events, speed is a basic factor.

What happens when a horse goes faster at the gallop? The beat is the same, but the horse "extends"—he lengthens stride, pushing more strongly from the rear quarters. This extension beyond the slow lope reaches its ultimate limit in the racehorse at full speed or in a jumping horse negotiating a high and wide obstacle. A racehorse's stride (complete three-beat cycle of the gallop) can be well over twenty feet in length.

When we move on from the slow lope, what we're doing is extending, lengthening the horse's stride. Now, we are not yet interested in real speed, only in a form of the gallop somewhat more extended than the slow lope. Conventionally, this next-more-extended variation is called the "ordinary" gallop or, to keep our terminologies consistent, the "ordinary" lope. It is not really fast; it is only a moderate lengthening of the horse's stride, but you'll be able to feel the difference.

It's not difficult to ask the horse to extend. You need simply to tighten your leg muscles. When you do this, you will feel the horse lengthen his stride under you. This transition ought to be smooth and supple; you don't want the horse spurting ahead, just calmly lengthening stride. There should be no commotion about it, no excitement. The feather-light mouth contact is preserved.

Accelerating out of the lope. The horse is lengthening stride quickly, but the rider's balanced position is undisturbed. He is slightly increasing rein pressure. The balance is admirable, permitting instant maneuvering.

The trickier problem is to come back to the slow lope from the ordinary lope. You are asking your horse, in this case, to shorten his stride. This transition is extremely important, because the ability to lengthen and shorten stride at will is vital to all reining work. You must be able to "accordion" the horse quickly and tactfully, eventually using the whole range of the horse's movements.

The transition back to the slow lope is accomplished primarily with the hand, of course. Like virtually all rein effects in western horsemanship, you will be asking the horse, not forcing him. The hand on the reins is gently squeezed or closed *in rhythm* with the beats of the gallop. The rein is not pulled or jerked back. The horse is "gathered," shortened, collected, "reassembled," by a contraction of the fingers, this contraction, this opening and closing of the fingers, done in harmony with the cadence of the gallop.[6] Normally, this shortening back to the slow lope takes two or three beats of the gallop, or two little squeezes with the fingers.

[6] I have used this odd word to describe the downward transition, because the French, quite logically, I think, actually use the verb *ressembler* to describe this process of gathering the horse.

86

What you must do now is to practice those transitions at the lope. Set your horse on the slow lope, extend into an ordinary lope, and then come back to the slow lope. When you can do this easily (without stress and with the transitions taking no farther than approximately the horse's own length), then mix these transitions with circle figures. From the slow lope cut a large circle, going into an ordinary lope as you begin the circle, and return to the slow lope as the circle is completed. Reverse the sequence; ride the ordinary lope and then cut a smaller circle, coming down to the slow lope on the figure, and then extend back into the ordinary lope as you come off the circle. You must be able to use the hand aid *both* for directional purposes (reining) and for transitions (shortening stride) simultaneously.

The more you work at these transitions, the fewer aids you will have to use. In a while, all you'll seem to have to do is to "think" lengthening and shortening and the horse will respond. This is a continuation of "instinctive" riding. Your thought will instantly convey the proper application of the aids. You will have a sort of ESP with your horse.

Riding any horse that performs, that is, does more than merely go around a ring, demands a decisive and alert mental attitude on the part of the rider. You must know what you want to do if these "instinctive" techniques are to be put to effective use. The indecisive rider, the one who moves his horse into performance situations with only a tentative, hesitant mental set, will soon convey this lack of concentration to the horse. The horse, in turn, will move hesitantly and sluggishly, uncertain of its tasks, lacking a vital nerve. Even in your private drills, then, practice the school figures with some intensity of mental concentration. Be decisive. Do it, and do it now!

Falling

Sooner or later the matter of falling is going to come up and this is as good a time as any to deal with it, since we're talking about "serious losses in balance." Fear of falling is a factor, large or small, in the psychological makeup of nearly all beginners. A good deal of the time it's irrational—either because the likelihood of a fall is exaggerated or the effects of a fall are similarly overblown. Falling off a horse need not be anticipated as an inescapable part of elementary instruction, but a fall can occur. The chances of being hurt (beyond simple bruises and aching muscles) from falling off a horse through a temporary loss of balance at the jog or slow lope in a riding ring are so remote as to be statistically irrelevant. The pace is slow, the ground even and relatively soft, the horse is not trying to dislodge you, and no hard objects (save the ring fence) are there to complicate your jeopardy. A fall from a horse covers a surprisingly short distance. Children, scrambling on and off horses, get used to tumbles, none of them much more severe than dropping off a kitchen stool and on softer ground. For children, some informal vaulting practice is an excellent way to conquer any misgivings they may have about a fall from a horse's back.

While a fall is not really something to look forward to, the thought of one ought not to inhibit your progress as a rider. Let me make two or three quick comments about falling: (1) There's no dishonor whatsoever in falling off. There's no "Code of the West" that implies you have to cling to the horse whatever happens. *If* you do lose your balance beyond recovery, bail out. (2) The best way to fall off a horse is in the "fetal" position: relax first, bring up your knees—elbows in, arms close to the body, head bent—like an embryonic ball. Not much will happen except getting your pants dirty. (3) More gravely, most serious equestrian accidents occur from the following circumstances: the horse falling; the rider striking some solid object (like jump equipment) during the fall; the rider being deliberately and violently thrown off by a dangerously unmanageable horse; collisions (between horses or with motor vehicles). Most of these hazards can be, with care and knowledge, avoided.

5

Using the Horse

We talked in the last chapter about a sort of ESP with your horse; in this chapter we'll try to refine it. We will shift our attention somewhat, from focusing on what you're doing to what the horse ought to be doing. This is simply realizing the goal of horsemanship: the performance of the horse. You now have the tools to work the horse instead of just being able to ride it.

We have two main objectives: performing more complicated school figures designed to introduce the art of reining; introducing some degree of speed into the work. In many larger western shows there are classes called "western riding." Those classes lie somewhere between "pleasure" classes (calling for walk, jog, and lope around the ring) and reining classes (requiring advanced movements like roll-backs, spins, and, also, speed). The elements in a western riding class are based on practical control and a certain amount of utility: changes of direction (and lead), gait transitions, simple patterns, and stops. These same elements are the ones with which we'll now be concerned.

The Figure Eight at the Lope

Having done changes of hand at the lope and figure eights at the jog, attempting the Figure Eight at the lope should not seem too unfamiliar. The major problems in doing the Figure Eight at the lope involve first, the maintenance of an even pace, and second, the pair of lead changes that occur as you cross the figure.

As with other figures, you'll want to begin with large figure eights, forty to fifty feet in overall length. Ride them first at the slow lope. At this size you'll have no difficulty at all in cutting the figure, the turns at the end not being very tight. The lead changes, however, will be a new experience. Earlier, you had come down to the jog and used your aids, but now you must merely cut the figure, letting the horse manage the change by himself. Chances are that the horse will change a little late; that is, he'll be almost into the turn before he switches leads. He may even (with a figure this large and the turns this broad) not change at all but "false gallop" the turn. Keep him going; don't rein up and impose a lead change on him. Later, with the figure smaller, he'll not "stick" on the lead changes. The change itself, when it comes, will surpise you—you'll get a slight jolting sensation, a mild twisting feeling.[1] It should not be disconcerting and, prepared for it, it won't bother you the next time.

The techniques involved in riding smaller and faster figure eights are best practiced on these larger figures, even if not all of these techniques are actually required. There are four important considerations: (1) In making the tight turns, the horse must have both impulsion and a strong engagement of the haunches. He'll need to be driven into these turns by *active* legs, a strong inside leg and a supporting outside leg to enforce the turn. The horse must be bent as much as possible on the turn.[2] (2) The hand must

---

[1] This sensation is caused by the fact that the stock horse does not make a dressage-type "flying" lead change, but changes first behind and then in front in a very rapid two-beat alteration of stride.
[2] Currently there is a very hot dispute in hippological circles about the extent to which the horse can bend his spine. The arguments on both sides are highly technical. I mention this only to point out that when we use the word "bend" in reference to the short-turning horse, we may be using the word in a figurative sense.

Loping a turn. Notice the secure and firm leg position with a slight commitment of weight to the left stirrup. The lateral inclination of the body is into the turn, square with the horse beneath. The hand has not been raised or pulled back; it remains supple and guiding.

not interfere with the horse's correct inclination to lower its head into the turn. This must be encouraged, even if the rider temporarily loses bit contact. The hand must be kept low and, in general, within the outlines of the body. (3) The rider's body must be deeply seated, weight proportionately distributed in the stirrups, but on the turns a greater amount of weight will go into the stirrups on the turning side. The body will incline slightly toward the direction of movement. (4) It is important to consider the Figure Eight as one fluid movement. You cannot break it up into segments. There is a rhythm about it that you must sense.

Regardless of mistakes that might occur, keep moving on the figure. Ride it as a continuous pattern.

In doing figure eights, some inexperienced riders have a tendency to lean away from the turns or raise the hand far too much, even to pull back or allow the lower leg to slip out of position, toe pointing down. Any one of these faults is serious enough to spoil the figure, to make the turns wrenching disasters. If you can avoid these problems during the figure eights done large and slow, you can begin to reduce the size of the figures. There is no need, though, to make the overall length of the Figure Eight less than twenty-five or thirty feet. Reducing size, you have to "help" the horse with your legs. If you don't, it's unlikely that you'll complete the figure at the lope, the horse losing impulsion on the tightened turns. With these smaller figure eights, it's a good idea to do two figures at a time, to link two figure eights together, thereby getting a strong sense of the rhythm demanded by the movement.

The Figure Eight is a very basic preparation for both horse and rider. It's like playing scales on the piano. Even if you're working a "made" cutting horse, say, you'll still be riding some figure eights. The figure not only encourages suppleness and balance, it constitutes an athletic exercise for the horse already highly supple and balanced.

Some of your figure eights can now be done at the ordinary lope. These quicker figures can be varied, too, by coming off them and allowing the horse to gallop away for a considerable distance. Later, as you'll see a bit further on, you can add a quick stop off the Figure Eight. Working at this increased speed, it is important not to get sloppy in your position or to become more aggressive with your aids than you need to be. Run a few figures and quit. Don't sour the horse, signs of which are fussiness with its head or resistance to the leg aids.

The Doubling Figure

In my opinion, the *Doubling Figure* is the most important preparation in the training of a reining horse. While we're not concerned here with training, that which forms a vital part of the horse's education frequently serves in the same role in the training of the rider. The essence of this chapter, this stage in your development, is *cooperation* between rider and horse in the preliminaries of performance, the successful mastery of particular testing movements. This cooperation is necessary in the Figure Eight and it is central to the ability to ride a doubling figure.

In a real sense this figure is really a series of figures; it is a basic movement with a huge number of possible variations. It is simple enough to diagram in its essential form:

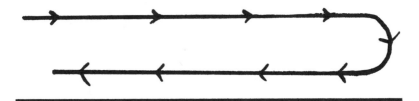

Doubling Figure

The principal variations of the doubling figure result from three factors: (1) the distance between the ring fence and the parallel course of the horse; (2) the speed at which various parts of the figure are ridden; (3) the distance involved in approaching the turn and moving away from it or, put another way, the overall length of the figure. Let's consider these factors:

(1) The distance between the ring fence and the parallel line taken by the horse determines the tightness of the turn, the "doubling back" of the horse into the fence. If you "double," for example, some thirty feet away from the fence, your turn will not be much tighter than a fair-sized half-circle not requiring the horse to pivot on his haunches. On the other hand, if you approach the turn about ten feet off the fence, the horse must make a very abrupt turn, forehand swinging, haunches pivoting, virtually a "roll-back" (which will be discussed in a later chapter). The ring fence, of course, is an integral part of this figure because it imposes a turn on the horse; by using the fence, you can predetermine, so to speak, the dimensions of the turn, the demands made on the horse. It will also accustom you, by the way, to turning sharply and quickly into the fence or arena side, necessary, as you'll see later, in stock-horse work.

(2) The doubling figure can and should be negotiated at all three gaits and at varying speeds. These gaits and speeds, as you'll discover in a moment, can be combined *within* the figure itself, as in the case, for example, when you might jog down parallel to the ring fence, turn or "double back" also at the jog, but then lope away once the horse is straightened next to the ring fence. The possible combinations that can be used are vast.

(3) You can make a long approach, like the entire distance of the long side of the arena, and double back just short of the corner, or you could make a very short doubling figure of only ten to twenty feet. Your approach to the actual "double-back" can be long or short and your progress away from it can also be long or short. For example, you could make a very short approach, double back, and then lope down the whole side of the arena, performing a quick stop in the corner.

These variations depend primarily on the levels of skill and experience enjoyed by both the horse and rider; some can be very easy and some can be extremely difficult. Remember that the doubling figure is a training device. Its use follows, therefore, a reasonable development, starting with the simple and progressing to the most demanding, as in contrasting some of the earlier examples I've mentioned and doing a very short double-back followed by "jumping out" the horse along the fence, all at speed.

Start, then, with a few very easy versions. Begin by working your horse about twenty feet off the rail and at the jog. Jog down, perform the turn, and jog back. Keep the whole progress even. Don't speed up going into the turn and, once turned on the track, stay close to the fence line.

The next variation involves jogging down, doubling back while still on the jog, and then, once the horse is straight on the track, immediately going into the slow lope. Slow lope down the long side of the arena with an even pace and rein up.

These first few variations (I've only mentioned two) are really familiarization runs to get you used to doubling and the problem of the turn. Before we move on to something more ambitious, a word or two about the aids is in order. The doubling figure, more than any other figure we've discussed so far, calls for the use of the "dwell." The leg must prepare the horse for the rein cue by being applied a fraction of a second before the hand aid. The effect is to lighten the forehand prior to sudden motion (like

Doubling back. The rider sits deep, but not away from the horse's thrust, the upper body slightly following the impulsion. The leg position must remain firm. Notice that the hand cues, but it does not force.

stops, spins, double-backs, and so on). Even at the jog, you might remind yourself to start employing the dwell, even if it has become, I hope, more or less habitual for you. In regard to the other effects of the aids, the double-back is executed in the same manner as the turns in the figure-eight pattern.

Now, then, you ought to try something more challenging. This time, jog down and *just before* the double-back pick up a slow lope, then immediately double into the fence at the lope and return down the side. You must be, of course, on the correct lead on the straightaway as you approach the double-back in order to manage the movement. For this reason, be extremely careful on your transition to the lope that you get the proper lead. If you've missed the right lead and are on the wrong one, pull up and start again. You don't want to try that double-back on a false gallop!

You will find this variation of the doubling figure considerably harder. Doubling just after the transition to the lope will invite the horse either to lose impulsion and "string out" on the turn or, conversely, to rush the double-back, to scramble, as it were. The harmony of the aids is the means by which you can preserve evenness and balance.

Don't cheat on the turns. Go deep into the fence. And don't drift off the track on the return trip. In order to get the benefit from the doubling figure, hug the fence line. At twenty feet off the fence, your horse doesn't have to "put out" much and you should insist that he turn close to the line of the fence. If he does scramble, now or later, sit down in the saddle, make sure his head is not interfered with, and let him sort himself out. In doing short figures, particularly at speed, any horse may at times put a foot wrong, seeming even to stumble. Your response to this is gentle support from your legs and granting the horse the freedom of his head. When a horse trips, there is a reaction on the part of the rider to snatch his head up. It is a faulty impulse. In order to regain balance, the horse must have the freedom to swing its head and the rider must release, not pull. A horse can go to its knees, even have all four quarters on the ground, and still recover balance and proceed on its way *if* the rider keeps his cool, sits in the middle of the horse, and doesn't snatch the reins.

By now you should be able to ride a doubling figure completely at the slow lope, still about twenty feet or so off the rail. Don't hurry; just keep the horse moving methodically under you. You will now feel the horse gather himself a little on the turn or double-back; he's beginning to push himself some with the haunches, engaged behind a bit more. Don't tip your body forward in response to this, but keep contact with your "sitting bones." Your upper body (from the hips) should now follow the arc of the turn *slightly*. Don't overdo this, but keep your trunk, above the hip line, supple and a little inclined toward the forward motion, in harmony with the horse's impulsion. The weight will be more pronounced in the stirrup on the turning side. The reining motion with the hand should be one quick, flowing gesture.

If you're pretty adept at this variation, you can now cut down the distance from the fence line by about five or six feet. It's not a bad idea to jog this shortened distance once, to get the feel of it. Things will happen a little faster, in the first place, and the horse will now have to lighten his forehand and use his haunches as a pivot to some extent. The problem at this reduced distance is to make a good doubling-back move, not flat and jerky or long and erratic. It should be a genuine half-circle. Go with the horse;

don't be "left behind" on the turn. The legs are still the key factor in the success of the double-back.

So far, you have been working at the slow lope. Stay on that pace until you're very smooth at the figure. Don't try to be too fancy too fast. When, however, you can double at the slow lope with consistent confidence and pretty consistent results, then add a new and crucial variation: "jumping out" off the double-back. This means performing the approach and the double-back at the slow lope, but then instantly accelerating as soon as the horse is straight on the rail. If done properly, the horse should accelerate so briskly, so instantaneously, that he appears to "jump out" or spurt ahead with a strong impulsion. To do it, you must ride the double-back firmly and quietly and then "ask" the horse with a quick, decisive closing of the legs. A trained stock horse will immediately understand this and will lengthen stride with a push from the haunches He needn't get excited, he merely "puts on the gas." What you want is *instant* acceleration, not a gradual lengthening over a stride or two. Your work with the doubling figure in general should have developed, perhaps unconsciously, a real boldness on your part, a quickness of response joined to a zest for immediate, split-second reactions from the horse. The "jump out" should display this boldness, this calm quickness. Shoot the horse ahead.

The next problem you can guess: riding the entire doubling figure at speed. Now you should not "jump out" off the double-back, but cut the whole figure at a pretty spritely ordinary lope. This is where the fun begins. The distance from the fence is still not great enough to force the horse to pivot on the haunches, "roll-back" in style, but it is short enough that you'll get a very exhilarating feeling of the horse "swapping ends" in a rapid, pivoting-like motion. It's your first feeling of what a stock horse can do. Be bold, sit deep, follow the motion, hug the fence.

The "graduation" version of the doubling figure is to ride the pattern at about the same speed, with the distance from the side of the arena shortened another five or six feet to about ten feet between your initial path and the fence line. This is close enough that the horse must half spin on his haunches. Again, try it first at the jog to get an impression of the measurement. Then slow lope it once or twice, "jumping out" as you come back. You'll notice

97

the need for aggressive leg aids on the double-back since the horse's impulsion is reduced by the fact that he's on the slow lope. The horse would actually prefer to do it with more momentum.

At increased speed, you'll have to swing the forehand of the horse, the haunches digging in and pivoting. The rein cue must be quick and feature a rapid but crisp use of the dwell. The dwell, as I've remarked before, involves a sequence of leg and hand aids that becomes not so much a matter of thought as simply an unconscious act. But in the case of more advanced reining movements, it is important that you take some care, devote thought, to "setting up" the horse with the dwell. This is crucial in performing a small doubling figure at speed. The horse's forehand must be prepared to rotate so swiftly that the double-back will seem to be one motion.

With these items on your mental checklist, try the figure. Stay against the horse's spine, your lower back braced as you go into the double-back. The forward momentum, the impulsion, must be maintained; the legs more than the hand turn the horse; the hand aid, once the dwell cue has been given, follows and confirms the turn.

The doubling figure in its variations is a major sphere of work. You can develop additional variations beyond those few I've outlined here. In using the doubling figure, don't repeat the same variation over and over again; mix them up. Be sparing on the use of speed; run the quick, small double-backs infrequently. Spend most of your time at the slow lope and even practice some at the jog. You want the horse instantly responsive if you ask for speed and very tight turns, but you don't want the horse to associate this figure wholly with the hard demands of the more taxing variations. If the horse gets this notion, he will tend to anticipate, to "bunch up" and get "nervy," excitable. Working slowly will also provide you with a better chance for self-correction, to analyze what you've done and to resist any temptations toward slipping into sloppy habits. When problems do arise, in the performance of either the horse or rider, the first thing to do is to go back to something more simple, something that you do well and confidently, and this will restore your mutual equilibrium, rider and horse.

The Across-the-Ring Serpentine at the Lope

The remaining work during this phase of your training will not emphasize speed but precision. You will be working at the jog and slow lope. The "Across-the-ring serpentine" is not a regular school figure but is a very helpful movement, more a simple reining pattern and one that is actually used, in a somewhat different version, in the program for "western riding" classes at horse shows.

Put three poles or oil drums along the long side of the arena, well off the ring fence and fifty feet or so apart. On the opposite side of the ring put two similar markers (poles or "barrels"), the same distance apart but located opposite the open spaces between the markers on the other side. Station yourself in the corner of the ring facing the row of three markers. Proceed along the rail until you just pass the first marker and then turn across the ring, aiming at the first marker on the opposite side. Half-turn around this marker, and then recross the ring and half-turn around the second marker on this side. Then go across the ring again to half-turn around the second marker and return to come inside the third or last marker, straighten up on the track, ride to the corner of the ring, and return to the walk.

You can see that this is a very big serpentine figure using the whole width of the arena. It is an easy matter to jog the horse through the pattern, but it's not so simple at the slow lope because you have four lead changes to make. The whole purpose of this pattern is to drill you and the horse on evenness of pace and smoothness in changing direction. The half-turns should be uniform, the pace steady, the angled tracks across the ring straight, the lead changes serene and unhurried. The horse will make the lead changes approaching the turns around the markers. Help him by a tactful cue with the inside leg, but don't swing him away from those markers. His head should stay down into the turns.

The Quick Stop

You have already made stops off the jog; now stops must be

made from the slow lope. This is not a "sliding" stop done from speed (which will be introduced later), only a smooth, precise stop executed from the lope, but it will form the foundation for the more flamboyant stops seen in reining-horse competitions. Once armed with the theory of the quick stop, the problem is to perform it without mistakes—the most common being a scrambling, jerky halt caused by the failure of the haunches to be properly engaged and initiating the stop, the horse's head up, fighting the restraint of the bit. You cannot expect to make a good stop from the lope until you can execute one from the jog that is instantaneous and smooth. The stop off the jog, then, should be repeated until you're able to stop on one beat, the haunches engaged, the head low. (You might well go back to earlier work suggested in Chapter Three.)

Let's analyze what happens when the horse stops. The stop begins in the rear, the horse engaging and lowering the haunches. The forehand, slightly raised, is braced, forelegs straight. The back of the horse is also straight; the head is flexed at the poll and lowered. In the true quick stop, the haunches are lowered to the point where the tail is on the ground, the hock even brushing the ring surface. The result is a short slide, the horse "braking" with the front shoulders and legs.

The beginning of the stop off the slow lope. Notice the horse commencing the stop by the engagement of the rear quarters, the forehand lightened, the head down and flexed. The rider's legs remain under the body, the back slightly braced, the hand kept low.

The stop from the slow lope should be abrupt but not violent. Excessive jerkiness in a stop results from the horse bouncing instead of sliding, this series of little bounces caused by an insufficient lowering of the haunches and stiffness in the forehand. The horse will not slide much stopping from the slow lope, but you will get the effect of a sliding action if you have executed the stop properly.

The key to doing the stop well is the rapidity with which you cue, use the hand and leg aids coordinating in a quick dwell effect and a halt cue. There are three primary ingredients in making a good stop: (1) the quickness, briskness, with which you follow the initial closing of the leg with the hand cue (the dwell cue); (2) the rapid, spring-like action of the hand (the halt cue); (3) the set of the rider's body. Quickness is more important than severity. A crude jab with the hand will only jerk up the horse's head. Set up the horse with the legs followed almost instantaneously with a decisive squeeze-pull with the reins, releasing at once. The cue with the reins must be definite and as quick as possible, as much like a coiled spring as you can make it. Bracing with the lower back is necessary both as a supplemental aid and a means of holding your position stable. Make sure your feet are pressed hard against the stirrup treads.

The difficulties you may have with the quick stop will follow from an unsatisfactory execution (causing an incomplete or ragged stop) or from defects in your position. If the horse does not in fact stop instantly, half-sliding, you have failed to communicate and the cue was slow and indefinite. If the stop was jerky, the horse resisting, it was probably the result of a lack of smoothness with the pull-and-release technique. A common fault is the failure of the horse to stop straight, his haunches going sideways. Active leg pressure must be used to keep the horse on the line and to put the haunches where they belong.

The most frequent embarrassment for the rider is getting pitched forward, chin on the horse's crest, or having the horse half go out from under, the rider's body jolted to the rear, sprawling over the cantle, legs on the "dashboard." In order to sit in balance during the stop—a very basic consideration—you must sit *tight*. The legs have to hold their position and the brace with the back must prevent the spine from rounding. You should not be hunched over at the completion of the stop. The less

101

movement of the body the better; you should give the impression that you're sitting still in the middle of the horse.

The most efficient way to practice this stop off the slow lope is to pick a spot in the ring, even draw a line across the track, where you intend to make your stop. Timing is critical; you want to stop where you want to stop. Count to yourself: "One, two, stop." This counting down to the stop may be helpful for a time or two; it will remind you of the need to use the dwell and to hit the stop quickly. You may find that you'll only succeed in doing "half-stops" at first, incomplete stops where the horse takes an additional step or two. This is caused by a lack of timing in your use of the aids. Keep at it. Doing the quick stop is like flipping pancakes; it's a knack, a dexterity, that will come to you only with a little practice.

Other Exercises

There are some additional maneuvers involving the stop that you can use profitably. Try this one: when you have halted, make sure that the horse stands quietly. Insist on that. Then, from the halt position, you can move directly into the slow lope again if your aids are exact enough. This halt-long-pause-move-off-at-the-lope sequence is a very useful exercise for both horse and rider. It can be made even more beneficial by the addition of three or four backing steps from the halt, so that the sequence will now go as follows: quick stop, long pause in halt position, back three steps, and then leave at the slow lope. It's a great gymnastic exercise for the horse, by the way, but it will also rigorously test your aids.

Also, the stop can be used in conjunction with the other figures we've been polishing up, like the Figure Eight, the across-the-ring-serpentine, and the doubling figure. Perform any of these patterns and then straighten away off the figure, adding a quick stop at the end. As a matter of fact, you can now link up some of these figures to form a short "reining pattern." For example: cut two figure eights at one end of the arena, then ride the across-the-ring-serpentine, and, finally, turn down the center of the arena and do a quick stop. You can make up your own combinations, but remember to vary the gaits in these improvised patterns. Combine walk, jog, and slow lope in different sequences. Make sure, by the way, that your horse is adequately warmed up before you attempt these patterns. Getting into faster work shouldn't mean that you've neglected a lot of slow, simple drill. You are rapidly arriving at the point where the patterns you're running are reasonably tiring on the horse, and consequently he shouldn't be asked to do many of them at one time.

Some Final Thoughts on Using the Horse

You can say now that you're "using" the horse, that it's becoming an instrument on which you can play. You are beginning to think less about "riding" and more about "doing." You yourself are starting to be able to detect "right" and "wrong" by the sensations the horse conveys to you. That network of nerves in your body is beginning to be conditioned. Frankly, the beginning stage is over, and you can commence to think about how you're going to get the most out of your horse.

You might think about this: if the problem of riding the fast, maneuvering horse at speed could be reduced to two basic principles, they might be these: (1) the need to remain close to the horse's center of gravity; (2) the development of instantaneous reactions to the horse's initiative—being "with the horse" at all times. These two factors are closely related, of course, and are not by now unfamiliar to you.

In riding the stock horse, the fact that the horse's center of gravity—located in the withers—shifts forward as the horse extends the length of his stride presents, in one sense, less of a problem to the stock-horse rider than to the rider of racehorses and jumping horses. The stock horse may extend his stride for brief periods, but, on the whole, his center of gravity does not move so far forward in his withers that the rider must radically change his position to adjust to it, as the jumping-horse rider and even the calf roper coming out of the chute must do. I believe that once you have an excellent basic position, the problem of remaining consistently close to the center of gravity depends to a large degree on using the proper saddle. The construction of the saddle will dramatically affect your ability to remain close to the withers and can reduce the possible movement of the lower body back and forth in the saddle.

At this point in your riding career, you must consider what you're currently sitting on and contemplate, if necessary, the acquisition of a suitable saddle. Too many stock saddles are excessively high in the front; they do not sit down on the horse's withers and these badly designed rigs keep you away from "where the action is." This defect results from saddles being built too narrow in the gullet, or with "swells" set too high, or with seats that angle down too steeply toward the cantle with the low point of the dip beyond the center of the seat. Conversely, a good saddle, suitable for stock-horse work, has a relatively flat seat, sits low in front, and has swells that do not push you away from the withers. The height of the cantles seems a big issue to many people, but in my system of horsemanship cantle heights are not very significant—because you don't lounge against the cantle in any case. In general, moderately low cantles are best, although for stock-horse use they may be somewhat higher than is conventional on roping saddles. The shape of the cantle is more important than its height. It should merge with the seat so as to be an extension of the dip. The cantle should not stick up from the saddle tree like the back of a chair. Ideally, too, a stock-horse-type saddle should have free-swinging fenders of not too thick leather, preferably set slightly farther forward than those on the traditional all-purpose saddle. Narrow stirrups—one- or two-inch treads—are recommended. And most people tend to buy stock saddles too long in the tree. Don't try to ride in a saddle where you've got a great expanse of useless space between your lower body and the swell fork; that, too, keeps you away from the center of gravity. Sitting on a badly designed saddle or one that doesn't fit your personal shape is like trying to hit a tennis ball with a juice strainer—it's frustrating.

The proper saddle will do two things: it will *help* you hold your position and allow you to get close to the horse so as to be more responsive to his movements. The best rig in the world, though, can't make up for a lack of instinctive response. That must be honed through exposure and repetition.

104

6

Games People Play

Since you are now beginning to use the horse, we can refine that ability and direct it toward more or less specific goals. These objectives, as you'll see presently, can be quite varied, but basically you are perfecting the art of maneuvering at speed and sharpening the controls. With the accumulated benefits of all that work on the school figures behind you, you should be able, now, to face much that is involved with reining, including the introduction of such things as quick stops off speed, roll-backs, spins, and other advanced movements.

More Complex Reining Patterns

From the standards of "western-riding" type work discussed in the last chapter, you must now consider these techniques expressly concerned with reining. The approach, in general, is still based on patterns, building toward the riding of more or less formalized reining patterns, such as those required in American Quarter Horse Association competition (see the appendix for examples of these). The preliminary patterns are of three types: (1) figure-eight patterns of various sizes at increased speed; (2) cloverleaf patterns; (3) pole patterns. There is nothing sacred about these particular patterns, but they are useful as preliminary exercises before you tackle a more regulation type of reining pattern.

You are already able to ride figure eights at the slow lope, so that the aim is to ride them with equal precision at increased speed, including the lead changes. Most "official" reining patterns call for two figure eights of differing sizes. A good exercise to begin with is to ride two relatively large figure eights of approximately equal size, the first one at the slow lope and the second at more speed. Then do two more figure eights at the speed of the second previous figure and finally two figure eights at speed with differing sizes. Don't try to do all of these in one sequence. Start with a pair of figure eights, loping the first and then galloping the second—not flat out but at a good, vigorous pace. This second figure will differ from the first in four principal ways: (1) greater quickness with the hand; (2) increased use of the leg aids; (3) greater need to shift weight into the stirrups on the turning sides; (4) greater "lean" of the horse on the turns, which requires a more flexible upper body, a more noticeable "going with" the horse with your upper body. At this speed the figure eight becomes a matter of timing, of rhythm with the aids (now including the body), if the figure is to be evenly and smoothly done. Also, the jolt of the lead change will be more pronounced and you will have to become accustomed to it by bracing the back. Don't swing the horse off line anticipating the lead change. You'll see this done once in a while, even in reining classes at shows, but it is neither necessary nor logical. Don't flex the horse *away* from the direction in which he's turning or beginning to turn. On the contrary, his head should be flexed and down *into* the turn. For example, the mark of a well-trained, barrel-racing horse is that it keeps its head flexed into the barrel and not away from it.

When you come to do your first figure eight at real speed, you must not hold back, unconsciously checking the horse into the turns. A common fault of the beginner in this situation is to feel the need to steady the horse (and perhaps himself) into the turns by slightly reining back and, then, to over-rein the horse on the turn itself, carrying the hand back instead of forward, as if to twist the horse's head around the circle. The time has come, to be blunt, to ride boldly. At speed, the figure eight cannot be broken into parts, as it were. It must be taken, swallowed, whole. It is

A turn at speed. The rider's legs do not move. The security of the seat permits a "free" hand on the rein. The rider, deep in the middle of the horse, remains close to the center of gravity. The "inside" leg invites the horse to flex.

The half-circle is a little trickier, in this position, than the double-back, because you don't have the fence to aid you in the turn and you must really hug the pole, the horse turning within his length. This requires a very strong inside leg contact, weight into the stirrup, and the body following the impulsion of the horse.

I'll sound like a broken record: don't overwork these figures—they're reasonably demanding on the horse. Try only a few during one practice session and, as always, intersperse the patterns with periods at the walk on slack reins and with slow repetitions at the jog in order to keep your horse from excitability and anticipation. You want the horse to be quietly responsive to your aids, but not tense and aggressive.

The Roll-back

In order to prepare for a full reining pattern, you must add the *roll-back*, the *spin*, the *quick* or *sliding stop*, and the *quick back* to your repertoire. The quick stop you have already had a go at from the slow lope. You have backed the horse slowly. The spin is a new movement. The roll-back, however, is essentially a doubling figure done at speed without the benefit of the ring fence. In the roll-back, the horse reverses direction at reasonable speed by turning on one beat of the gallop, the forehand lightened to the extreme, and then resumes the rhythm of the gallop in the opposite direction. In judging roll-backs performed under competitive conditions, three main factors are particularly noted: (1) that the horse is not excessively checked prior to the movement; (2) that the forehand is really off the ground, the pivot truly on the haunches; (3) the horse moves away with a strong, even beat at the gallop. These criteria are useful in appraising the technique involved in riding the roll-back. The poorest approximation of the roll-back is when the horse really performs just a tight turn rather than a genuine pivot on the haunches. The key to the well-performed roll-back, then, is an almost split-second lightening of the forehand, the haunches deeply engaged under the horse, permitting a quick doubling back virtually within the horse's length.

This must be attained by precise cueing. As in the doubling figure, try your first roll-back at a slow lope and down the center of the arena. Before you commence the figure, decide in which direction you're going to roll-back; you must be, then, on the correct lead as you come down the center, a left lead if you're going to roll-back to the left, and vice versa. Pick some spot on the ground as a target. Approach this point evenly, but it is not necessary that you hit it exactly, only approximately. Far more important—and infinitely more difficult—is trying to time your cue for the roll-back so that you actually ask for it (leg and hand) at the beat of the horse's galloping stride when the correct forefoot is off the ground—left for the left roll-back and right for the right roll-back. This is easier to say than to do, don't kid yourself about that. A lot of the time you'll miss doing this, but it should be kept foremost in your mind, because only in this way will you finally develop a sense of the horse's galloping cycle and the precise timing involved in delivering your roll-back cue, the dwell and the rein cue.

Approaching the turning point, trying to cue when the correct forefoot is off the ground, you must employ the dwell followed by a fast rein effect in the desired direction. Step immediately into the turning-side stirrup as the forehand comes around and then close both legs, the upper body canted slightly forward, leaning into the roll-back. Don't overdo this; the forward inclination is only a very few degrees. The problem is that all of this will happen far faster than it takes you to read the sequence of events. The roll-back is one complete movement. It should be done without stress and strain, but with real boldness. In this connection, don't check the horse before the turn by noticeably reining back; you can "gather" the horse for the roll-back sufficiently only by a contraction of the fingers in the dwell cue. On the well-trained horse, the vital and sudden "collection" for the roll-back can be gained without a forceful pulling on the horse's jaw. The lightening of the forehand is the result of training and not the rider's intervention of force. If the roll-back is well executed and done with calmness, the horse will lope away from it without plunging forward. As with most tight figures, it is wise to watch the horse's head; it is a prime indicator of how well things are going. The horse should not shake its head or lay its ears back. The head should be low and slightly flexed toward the turn. The rein contact should convey to you almost a feeling of limpness, certainly no feeling of tenseness.

111

Having run a few roll-backs at the lope, you can try one at increased speed. The technique is exactly the same, but the suddenness of the doubling back off an accelerated pace puts some pressure on your ability to stay deep in the saddle. You must keep the sitting bones against the seat of the saddle. The best way to do this, of course, is to flex the muscles of the lower back going into the roll-back, even as you ever so slightly incline forward from the hips. But this flexing of the lower back—and the *lower* back only—ought not to make the whole upper body rigid. A stiffness in the upper body may cause you to be behind the horse on the double-back, even leaning away from the turning side. You can't expect to hold the upper body absolutely still while doing these more advanced reining patterns; there will be a sort of whiplash response, but it must not only be kept in bounds but also used to assist balancing. The alternative to an awkward stiffening of the whole upper body is a secure balance from the stirrups—and with added weight temporarily in the stirrup on the turning side. With these principles in mind and after some practice, you'll find that roll-backs off some speed will not cause any feelings of loss of control.

The Spin

The spin consists basically of a three-hundred-sixty degree turn on the haunches, a pirouette figure well known to those familiar with dressage. The difference between the spin of the reining horse and the turn-on-the-haunches of the dressage horse is in the speed with which the figure is performed, beyond the fact, of course, that the cueing is radically different. The spin is a spin; the horse pivots quickly on its haunches, returning to its original position after coming around the full three-hundred-sixty degrees.

In theory, the effort made by the horse, in rudimentary terms, is similar in the spin and the turn-on-the-haunches. The haunches engage, the forehand lightens, the rear quarters serve as a base upon which the horse pivots. As a matter of fact, I use the turn-on-the-haunches, dressage-style, in training as a preparation for the spin. However, beyond this basic similarity, there are crucial differences; the spin is quick, the quicker the better, and the cueing is almost completely different (as between a "direct" rein and a "neck" rein system). We are concerned here with how to ride the spin and not how to train the horse to do it, so we must assume that the horse you're on can perform a spin if you provide more or less orthodox cueing.

Preliminary to beginning to ask for the spin, alert your horse. A slight squeeze with your leg and a contraction of your fingers on the rein will get the horse on his mettle. He must be prepared and poised to spin. Remember that you're beginning your spin from a halted position; the hope is that these little preparatory aids will cause your horse not only to be alert and ready but also to stand square on his legs. You must learn to spin in both directions, but start with a spin to the left. The sequence of cues and aids should be as follows: ask the horse to make a step forward—in reality a half-step—invoke the dwell, close both legs, and then flutter the inside spur *at the same moment* that you rein to the left (in performing the spin to the left). Swing the horse in a complete circular pivot, holding the rein against the opposite neck and keeping up that *tremolo* effect with the spur.

Don't be surprised if the first time you try this you get what is in reality a one-hundred-eighty degree turn on the haunches, the horse seeming to "stick" when he is in fact facing in the opposite direction, and you have to supply a second cue. This difficulty results from the fact that the necessary lightness of the forehand has not been sustained and the horse needs to pause to set himself and relighten his front end. This is likely because the haunches either have moved ahead or have swung to the side, therefore not serving as a base for the movement. The way to correct this is to make sure that your legs hold the haunches in position and that the spin is done with a quick, continuous motion. It can't be done in slow motion, so to speak. There is no way to practice the true spin at half speed. It must be a fast, uninterrupted pivot; the horse can't manage it any other way.

The Quick Stop

The difference between the "quick stop" you've practiced off the slow lope and the stop you must use in reining patterns lies in the fact that the stop off speed will involve a true *sliding* stop. If you can ride a good stop from the lope, you can do the same when you stop from a faster gallop, provided that the abilities of the horse are equal to it. A beautiful quick stop in competition contains all the elements of a less flamboyant stop made from the slow lope; the horse's head is low and flexed, the back is straight, the haunches initiate the stop, extremely low, hocks underneath the horse. The added feature is the sliding effect that follows from the abruptness of the halt made against the vigorous impulsion of the horse—as if a blow from a man's fist was halted in midair, not by a solid wall, either, but by an invisible soft curtain of control. The horse, obedient to the cue, himself checks his forward progress, skidding like a car braking on slippery ice, except that the horse is sliding on the softer going of the ring surface.

While the cueing involved is the same as was previously described for a stop, there are some additional requirements on the part of the rider: (1) the rein cue must be still quicker and, possibly, more forceful; (2) the impact of the stop is much greater, demanding a really strong use of the lower back to prevent being pitched forward; (3) it may be necessary to assertively use the leg aids to keep the horse straight during the stop; (4) it may also be necessary to provide a secondary hand cue as the horse slides over a fair distance. The initial rein cue that signals the stop may need to be subtly repeated in order to hold the horse in the stop position if the slide is of any duration. You get a brief "glide" sensation in doing the stop off the slow lope, but this is much more pronounced in the true quick stop. Sitting properly, it is a pleasant experience; you are close to the horse's spinal column, and the forehand is flexibly raised in front of you.

The quick stop can be practiced gradually. Work up from stops off the slow lope to those at increased speed, a little at a time. Stopping is hard on a horse, so don't attempt very many at one time. Watch the head for signs of irritation and resistance. The horse should not pull you, incidentally. A tired horse, however, will resist the cue and lug against your reining hand. Any difficulties with the quick stop should be met in the standard manner; reduce the speed involved and after some diverting slow work try a few stops from a much slower pace.

Quick Backing

The stock horse should be able to really fly to the rear for reasonable distances, if asked. Watch a rope horse work a rope or a reining horse doing a quick back. The movement is straight, even, and rapid with no signs of stress or strain. This results from intensive training, like the spin. The average horse, taught to back, cannot, except with much additional work, perform this movement. The cueing for the quick back is, once again, basically the same as for the slower back, but the rein cue is quicker—a series of rapid, pulsating little tugs. The legs are gently engaged against the horse's barrel, and leg pressure, left or right alternately, encourages the horse to back straight. A flutter or two, very lightly, with the spur is sometimes needed. Make sure, again, that the rein cues are tactful enough so that the horse's head is not forced to jerk upward. Any backing movement, slow or fast, that is done with the horse's head in the air is awkward and erratic. Backing is a physically taxing movement for a horse and should be done sparingly.

Back to Reining Patterns

To sum up, the standard features of reining patterns are figure eights, quick stops and backs, roll-backs and spins. You might take a glimpse of the examples in the appendix. Ordinarily, the figure eights are done first, the stops and spins introduced later. There is no reason now why you can't try a complete reining pattern, even one taken directly from the rule book. These patterns need not be done in practice at quite the tempo you'd use in the show ring (with the exception of the spin which, I believe, cannot be done well unless it's executed as quickly as possible).

To run a good reining pattern means "putting it all together." That is, the pattern should not be so much a series of figures as it should be one even, flowing performance, each movement linking smoothly into the next, creating the impression of control, economy, and grace. I think a good performance of any kind is characterized by the impression made on the spectators that the performer is never operating at his full capacity, that his technique is so finished it allows for even greater virtuosity than he displays. This is particularly true of a first-rate riding exhibition where a "course" of figures or obstacles is involved (as in reining or in jumping). Things should look, in other words, well in hand at all times, the rider showing no trace of being frantic, unsure, or lacking in confidence. In reining patterns, it is necessary to know where you're going, quite literally. You should plan exactly where you're going to make your figures and moves in the ring. The pattern, clear in your head, should be transferred to the ring area. In preparing for competition, ride parts of the standard pattern and then combine the parts into a full-blown run, a rehearsal, concentrating on linking the movements evenly.

Riding the Trail

To keep our work concentrated, we have been working in the ring. It is, after all, the "classroom." But as soon as you can walk, jog, and lope securely and confidently, it's a fine idea to leave the ring periodically and hit the trail. Riding "outside" is usually a bit of a surprise to the beginning student. "Outside" seems so spacious, and even quiet horses are a bit more prompt and alert out of the ring. Students as well as horses can become "ring sour," though, and riding the trails is a necessary part of your education anyway, if for no other reason than that trail riding introduces the element of the unexpected, ranging these days from encounters with jackrabbits to motorcycles.

There is nothing drastically different about riding a horse outside a ring. For a short time, perhaps, the uneven footing takes getting used to, going up and down undulations in the ground. The main difference is that on the trail or cross-country you should always be looking ahead of you, anticipating anything that might unsettle your mount. You can relax on the trail, but don't go to sleep, as it were, because a certain amount of defensive alertness is highly recommended. There are few horses that will not spook at something and it is truly amazing what you may run into in the great out-of-doors. I remember, once, riding deep in the Superstition Mountains of Arizona in rough terrain and miles from anyone, and out from behind a clump of Palo Verde trees, only a few feet away, pops a guy on foot! A solitary backpacker. A desert-bred horse may stroll past a sidewinder (rattlesnake)

116

without a quiver, but a hot-air balloon rising in front of him might be something else again. Don't take any horse for granted. Know your horse's peculiarities. I had a palomino mare once that was broke to death—your Aunt Ethel could ride her—but never hang a canteen filled with water on her saddlehorn! One of the best school horses I've ever owned would demurely lie down and roll in any sizeable body of water he came to if the rider didn't hurry him along a little.

You will discover, out on the trail, why you spent so many hours in the ring learning the slow jog. That is the real trail gait and, once you're really balanced, you can go for long distances at it with substantial comfort. A good trail rider, though, will copy the cavalry's old system; he'll vary the gait, walk a while, jog for a spell, and then let the horse lope along for a distance and then repeat the cycle, using the walk, though, more of the time than the other gaits.

Disobedience

The main purpose of this discussion is to prepare you mentally for some of the unexpected occurrences that you might have to face. Horses shy for one of two reasons: they are genuinely startled by something or they are showing resistance, "trying" you, not being too keen about getting on with the job. It's not too difficult to tell the difference between these two actions. A startled horse will jump, often snort, quiver, stiffen. Usually the cause is pretty evident. A resisting horse will shy for no reason at all, not quite so quickly, and may occasionally "swap ends" or half rear or "crow hop" in the bargain.

Your response to a frightened horse is to stay in the saddle, check him, quiet him, and, if necessary, encourage him not to back up. Most horses will, if gently urged, move up toward whatever spooked them and once getting used to it move on past or over without much additional fuss. Sometimes a genuinely frightened horse will simply not respond, say, to urgings that he cross a creek or a bridge, or he will become sufficiently terrified by something (perhaps a gang of motorcycles, a piece of farm machinery, or a loud explosion) that he will blindly bolt or rear. In my opinion, under these circumstances, there is no dishonor in

117

dismounting; it's sensible. There's no profit in trying to cope with a horse unresponsive to your control, and on foot you can lead up to or over something the horse wouldn't tolerate with you on his back. It may take a little time and patience, but he'll finally come to it. Horses are not remarkably bright, as I've mentioned before, but they have excellent memories and, in most cases, when a horse has learned that some object won't hurt him, he'll accept it afterwards when he confronts it or something like it again. He sort of files the experience away for future reference.

The horse that tries shying in order to resist is another matter. He may be just testing you a little or he may be seriously attempting to put you on the ground, but both notions are not to be tolerated. The trouble is, frankly, that a crafty, roguish horse can come close to putting you off balance, at least at a real disadvantage. Hang on. Stay with him the best way you can, using your leg grip as an emergency measure. Keep his head up, even with a jerk of the rein. A quick snatch with the reins *(unless* the horse is rearing) will "get his attention" and, since horses are single-minded you can frequently distract them. If you're pretty well seated, punish him swiftly with the legs (and spurs), driving him forward even if he plunges ahead. Whipping him with a quirt or a crop isn't much good, and never hit a horse with the reins.[1] The most effective punishment is with the legs. Rein him in the original direction and move him on briskly. That, in most cases, will end the rebellion.

Horses will buck, too. They buck for a variety of reasons. Sometimes bucking is an expression of good feeling or excitement; sometimes it's one of fear. Sometimes it is a form of resistance (the horse is tired, sore, or resentful of rough treatment), sometimes he's trying to dump you, and sometimes he's learned how to get away with it and to use it to intimidate people. Occasionally, but rarely, there are horses that are "just plain ornery." Horses buck in different ways, too, from a relatively mild elevation of the croup to all four feet off the ground, head

[1] I'm not very keen on whips. The trouble is that the horse's ability to connect cause and effect is very short, a matter of a second or two, and usually a rider takes longer than that in order to regain enough balance to use the whip, to punish the horse with it. Hitting the horse, then, has no real purpose. The legs (spurs, too) are quicker and more effective. I use a quite long whip occasionally to reinforce the leg aids in working with very green stock, carrying the whip so that it falls just behind the calf of the leg.

down, back arched. No riding student, perhaps even any sensible person, ought to have to cope with a confirmed bucker. These animals are "criminals" we won't discuss. But you may have to deal with the horse that puts in a buck because he "feels so good he hurts" or because he's momentarily frightened or because he wants to make a gesture of illegitimate resistance.

The best reaction to a single buck by a young, good-feeling horse or a horse expressing a fleeting spasm of excitement is to do nothing. Stay with him and pretend it didn't happen and get on with the business at hand. If you make a "federal case" out of it, you're apt to encourage him to buck again. Usually these exhibitions of spirit aren't all that difficult to sit to if you have a good position, and you don't need to invoke special measures.

But the horse may buck more energetically because he's spooked or resistant. In this case, do two things: try to keep the horse from getting his head down, jerking his head up if necessary, and drive him forward. The horse has difficulty in bucking if he can't bring his head down to about knee level; he must also pause for an instant to place his front feet and if you can keep him going forward, it's harder—but, alas, not impossible—for him to buck. If you're able to ride out the buck (caused by whatever), don't stop the horse and reflect on your victory. Keep him moving, take him back to work, cut a few school figures even if you're out on the trail, assuming you can find some open ground. Of course, be alert now in the event that he'll try it again. Most horses, except for real crafty bronks, "signal" a buck ahead of time. You can feel them bunch up underneath you and get ready. This is the time to move them on, divert their minds, and indicate you're not in the mood for nonsense.

Rearing can be an incurable vice. A confirmed rearer is a dangerous animal and not worth fooling with. Some horses will rear, however, primarily out of fear or mild displeasure. Horses that rear for no reason at all, except sheer defiance, are questionable items, and such continued activity may mean the need to "send them down the road," as they say. Some forms of resistance are less serious; some horses may rear, for example, as a part of the "barn rat" syndrome, resisting going away from the stable or corral. Anyway, there are really two forms of rearing: the first is more accurately a half rear, the horse's forehand coming off the ground, but the horse's balance is not in jeopardy;

119

the second form is dangerous because the horse really goes up in the air, balancing precariously on his hind legs, his back almost perpendicular to the ground. A horse in this stance can very well come over backwards. Horses that display this second type of rearing are either accomplished rearers seriously trying to do you damage or are deeply terrified horses that have temporarily lost their sense of self-preservation. Both are chancy.

React to a rearing horse by slacking the rein. A sudden rearing motion, catching you unawares, may cause a sense of loss of balance that you may try to compensate for by grabbing the reins. Don't. A hurriedly tightened rein, in this predicament, might cause the horse to come over backwards and it's disconcerting, to say the least, to have a thousand pounds of horse in your lap or, worse, on top of you. Next, drive him ahead vigorously; he can't rear or hold a rearing position if you force him onto his forehand. In extreme cases, it may also be sensible to throw your arms around his neck in order to prevent yourself from slipping backward over the rear of the saddle onto the croup if the horse is really up on his hind legs.

Confirmed runaways are rare. You shouldn't be mounted on one. There are horses, though, that when excited are apt to become strong, pull, and get rank at a pretty decent clip at the gallop. To be frank, it's awkward to deal with a runaway under western equipment with the customary aids; the western mode of reining is not very well suited to dealing with headstrong horses. Don't misunderstand; there are numerous successful means in western horsemanship to cure this vice by training, but I'm referring to the problem of dealing with the horse that is running away with you unexpectedly, with ordinary tack on him. *If,* consequently, you're convinced that you've got a really rank horse on your hands, that he's out of control at the gallop, go to a two-handed, direct-rein technique with full contact with the horse's mouth. Don't attempt to stop or pull up the horse with a steady pull on the reins—the harder you pull, very likely the harder he'll run. Move your hands back and forth with the arcing motion of the horse's head, closing the fingers firmly on the reins as the hands are drawn back. This technique will attempt to shorten the stride. If, gradually, the stride is shortened, in nearly all instances you can bring a horse back under control. By all means, too, turn the horse if you can, pulling him up in a tight circle finally.

If you've got plenty of room with safe footing and you're anxious to teach the horse something, let him run. He won't run forever and after a time he'll begin to tire; running off won't seem nearly as exhilarating. When this happens, don't let him slow down, but make him keep at it. Making him gallop for a while, tired, you can easily pull him up and he'll be a lot less anxious the next time to take you for a wild ride. If you have an over-keen horse that really wants to be aggressive with you, gallop him some on soft going, like sand or ploughed fields, not only to take his "top" off, but also to teach him some respect for your control. Up and down inclines is useful, too.

There are several other theories about how to deal with runaways, some of them downright picturesque. Some of them work, too, but the methods described above are pretty successful unless you have some iron-jawed rogue. If you're riding in company, by the way, *never* chase a runaway (despite the gallant scenes in Hollywood films). Chasing the culprit will only encourage him to run that much faster and farther. Pull up your own mount and wait. It sounds hardhearted, but chances are good that the runaway will go for a distance and then his herd instincts will take over and he'll want to rejoin the other horse.

There are a lot of other unpleasant under-saddle vices that horses may have, like refusing to leave the barn area, trying to brush off the rider against trees and fence posts, even lying down. Some horses will kick at their own kind and hit you in the bargain. Watch out for laid-back ears and lowering croups. Some horses are "nigglers"; they won't do a flat-footed walk and will jig up and down at a stiff trot all the time or even prance sideways. Sometimes horses like this can be "remade" and sometimes they can't. In any event, these problems are really beyond our objectives in this book and they don't call for special riding techniques beyond those you've already acquired. It is sensible, though, if you plan to do a lot of trail riding to make certain your horse is surefooted. Beware of too much stumbling, particularly at the lope. Some crack "rock" horses (horses that are agile in rocky, steep terrain) seem to stumble a good deal at the walk on flat going, but they are like goats in rough country. A horse that stumbles at the lope needs looking at. He may be shod wrong or he may be unsound. You don't want a horse coming down with you; that's bad news.

Some Quick Trail Tips

Most of ordinary trail riding is gaining experience. There are a few simple rules that might be helpful. Check your tack every now and again; a slipped saddle can cause a sore back. Carry a hoof pick and check feet, too. Look out for little stones or pebbles wedged against the frog. Don't go off the walk on really hard surfaces. Lean forward going *both* up and down steep inclines. If you're out for many hours, it may be comfortable to drop your stirrups down a hole or two. If the horse urinates on the trail or makes manure, stand in your stirrups and relieve the pressure of your weight near his kidneys while he's so engaged.

Other matters are more technical and controversial. The real art of trail riding is to maintain the condition of the horse and there are numerous ways of doing this, some of which are open to honest dispute, by the way. For example, I am generally against loosening the cinch during fairly short rest periods, but many excellent trail riders, more traditionally, adhere to the practice. I like sheepskin cinch covers, but many trail hands despise them, and so on.

Spend as much time as you can in the open. It's good for you and the horse. Ring drill is vital, but so is the natural cooperation of horse and rider on the trail, plains, or mountains. Riding through the quiet of remote country is one of the rewards of your training, to say nothing of constituting one of the last practical forms of escape from the "urban-industrial age."

Different Games to Play

When you get to the stage of riding reining patterns, you are at that point in your horse addiction when some choices arise in regard to specialization. You are no longer a beginner—except in terms of the specialization you may select. What do you do with your newly acquired skill? In western horsemanship these choices boil down to five main areas: (1) stock horses (reined cow horses and cutting horses); (2) show-ring riding (pleasure, trai , reining—also showing at halter); (3) trail riding (endurance, competitive, or just informal); (4) roping (calf, steer, and team events); (5) gymkhana or "gaming" (barrel-racing, pole-bending. and a host of other events). These areas are not mutually exclus ve and many riders' activities overlap the categories. Many breed exhibitors show their horses both "Western" and "English" (hunt or saddle seat) and drive, as well. Versatility is wholesome, I think, but still it is necessary to channel one's interests.

The principles of horsemanship we've been exploring are applicable to all these areas, and two specific ones—showing and stock-horse riding—will be considered in the next two chapters. Reining ability (man and horse) is important in the first, second, fourth, and fifth areas in varying degrees. The second and third areas feature events that can be rather casually pursued, while the first, fourth, and fifth are reasonably athletic in their de nands. The fourth area means the cultivation of another quite d fferent skill—throwing a rope. There are team events in the first, fourth, and fifth. Some of these activities are quite formal, others very informal and spontaneous; some can be distinctly expensive, some are very modest in cost. Top professionals in the first and fourth areas can collect substantial prize money. In the third and fifth and, to some extent, the second, you can have fun on a pretty inexpensive horse. The superior animals and training requ red for the first and fourth categories and the "big time" in the second make your horse investment far more substantial. Very r gorous performance training is involved in some of these arees, particularly the first, second, and fourth, which call for either a good deal of skill and experience yourself or a professional rainer. There is no doubt that "showmanship" plays a role in the show ring, but that doesn't suit everyone's temperament. Many serious horsemen, especially those involved with the first and second, don't think much of the fifth, but many people, on the other hand, like the informality and relaxed atmosphere of gymkhana events. People involved in the third category are very dedicated, and for those who are not ring-oriented this is the area where horse and environment happily meet. There are regional aspects to these specializations, too. Showing is nationwide, along with gymkhana; trail riding of varying types is now widespreac across the country. Stock-horse and roping interests tend to be more common in cattle-raising regions; also, these areas tend to be almost completely Quarter Horse-dominated (although many Appaloosa and Arabian fanciers are in this game, too). All breeds show and trail ride, and non-purebred horses are common in gymkhana and "open" horse shows.

This may be an endless subject. The above comments are strung together with a view to giving you a hasty idea of what further interests you might develop. Showing horses and trail riding concentrates on the horse itself; stock, roping, and gymkhana horses are trained "tools" used in more game-like situations. Either you will develop a strong interest in one or more of these "games" or you will be content, quite justifiably, to merely enjoy your companionship with the horse.

A word about risk. Aside from rodeo, western horsemanship is not a particularly risky business (as contrasted, in degree, with polo or jumping). Well-mounted, western events are not dangerous despite their frequent speed and dash. There are certain minimal risks in events calling for the use of cattle (roping, particularly) and some gymkhana events (particularly those not too well planned and supervised) that pose some hazards, but on the whole nearly everyone can take part in western horsemanship events without a Blue Cross subsidization.

Let's take a look, then, at a few of these areas of specialization you might choose to "graduate" into.

Care of the Performance Horse

This book is limited to equitation and does not extend into training and horse management. However, since you're involved in fairly advanced work with your horse, I'm inclined to say a word or two about the general care of the performance horse, an animal expected to do hard and fast work. I make a point of this, because while people understand that special care of one sort or another has to be given to racehorses, jumpers, and polo ponies, too often stock horses, while not neglected, are not given the extra attention that the type of work they do suggests or even demands. Stock-horse work puts pressure on horses and that ought to be acknowledged.

All performance horses must be *slowly* walked down after strenuous work.[2] If the horse is really hot, the coat wet and the body temperature obviously higher than normal, I advocate that the horse be walked a little to get his breathing normal, and then be given a sponge bath with a mixture of warm water and a dash of commercial liniment such as Bigeloil or Absorbine. This mixture, when applied, produces a pleasant and stimulating "wash" like an alcohol rub for a human being. After this quick sponging, put a cooler over the horse and walk him dry, either by leading him on foot or in a mechanical "hot walker." While he is "walking down," still warm and with pores open, I recommend that you give all four legs a brisk rub with a good liniment cut with alcohol. This procedure not only has a mild analgesic effect on possibly strained and sore muscles, but the act of rubbing the legs will provide a routine opportunity for you to inspect the legs. Horses working at speed are susceptible to a host of leg problems, some major and some minor, such as tendon and ligament strains, windpuffs and even splints, and you should detect these rapidly so that you can take prompt remedial action. Check the feet, too, for hoof cracks, loose shoes, abrasions on the heels. Clean the foot out with a hoof pick while you're taking a look. You might keep in mind that some ninety percent of all causes of unsoundness occurs below the knee on the front legs. Keep an eagle eye on them.

You can substitute a full bath for the sponge bath, using a good grade horse shampoo. But a word about baths is in order. I don't like to bathe a horse every day as that washes out the natural oils in the coat. For too many people, a "hose bath" becomes an easy substitute for grooming with a rubber comb and a dandy brush, grooming necessary for the horse's health. Two times a week for baths is adequate or even maximum. Never bathe in really cold water (it doesn't have to be bath-rub temperature but the chill should be taken off) or when the weather is cool (unless you have an indoor wash rack). Don't forget to sponge the muzzle, nostrils, and tail dock. Geldings should have their sheathes bathed

---

[2]Some polo enthusiasts are currently abandoning the practice of walking ponies between chukkers and prefer to let them stand on the picket line. This procedure was propounded by a veterinarian who is also a well-known poloist, Dr. Billy Linfoot, and he has some interesting arguments in support of this method. I remain old-fashioned and favor walking hot horses.

occasionally. Unless the weather is downright hot, walk the horse dry under a cooler. Be sure to rinse the soap out of the coat and scrape away the excess moisture. A "cream rinse" is sometimes good to use on manes and tails.

Diet, too, is a complex subject outside the scope of this book, but I will add a brief comment: it is impossible to discuss adequately or prescribe on this subject without a thorough knowledge of what the horse has actually been fed, where the feed comes from, and the explicit nutritional situations in the immediate locality where the horse is maintained. Talk over the problems of nutrition with your veterinarian. In general, I see little use for expensive dietary supplements of various sorts *unless* they compensate for some real deficiency in the diet brought about by local conditions (quality of the hay, lack of minerals in the soil, etc.). Grass remains the horse's natural forage and is also a splendid tonic; not enough performance horses are allowed a chance to get at grass these days. Find some grass and a halter shank and take your horse out to graze when you can.

The stock horse is an athlete and should be fed and exercised like one. If you're serious about training and conditioning, I urge you to keep a "log" (in a book or a tag-board sheet in the tackroom) with daily entries so that you can not only plan what your horse ought to be doing but also note what you, in fact, did. Supplementary information on shoeing, vet's examinations and treatments, innoculations, and feeding schedules can be included. Horses cannot be just fed the same amounts day in and day out, by the way. In training, the horse's diet may have to be adjusted *daily* according to the work done.

One final observation: permit your horse to regularly exercise *at liberty*. There are sound reasons, physical and psychological, why horses need freedom to play, if only for a few minutes per day. Aside from this, it's a delightful interlude for the owner or trainer if you've got the time to stand and watch. This may not be wasted time, either. I believe you can learn something about a horse by observing it at liberty. Of course, the horse will very likely roll—that's a natural urge he'll indulge—and he'll get dirty as a result, but that's a small price to pay for improving his outlook on the world.

126

7

Throwing Your Hat
in the Show Ring

Through the years, I have had a long stream of students who have firmly announced at the outset of their instruction that all they wanted to do was to ride well enough for their own private enjoyment. There's nothing wrong with that motivation, but a large majority of those who made this proclamation were eventually tempted to try their skills in horse showing. While the ultimate satisfaction in horsemanship is without doubt the solitary awareness of accomplishment, the lure of the show ring is very understandable. I suppose one of the reasons for this is that in all phases of our lives competition, of various kinds, is emphasized and skill seems to imply, in itself, some eventual public, competitive exhibition. Even golfers who struggle to break a hundred want to play in tournaments. But the more solid impetus to enter the show ring arises, I think, from the social aspect of the sport— and by "social" I don't mean any snobbish inclination to join the so-called "horsy set." This social aspect is a companionship, a sharing of the intense addiction to working with horses. The horse show, currently, is a fascinating blend of the vestiges of the medieval tournament, an old-fashioned "barn-raising," and a cult ritual all rolled into one. But the most prominent feature of it is the coming together of people of like interests and dispositions in an atmosphere of both competition and a more easygoing interchange of experiences.

Of course, there is a commercial side to horse showing. The "horse industry" has enjoyed a breathtaking growth in recent years and horse shows have become big business as a result. Larger shows tend to be dominated by professionals and regrettably even "amateur" events are often masterminded from the sidelines by shrewd professionals. In some areas of horse showing, this professionalism has reached such levels of competitive intensity, to say nothing of the money involved, that the bona fide amateur might well become permanently disenchanted if he still pursued fun as a primary objective. Happily, this is less true of western showing in general, and the wide variety of horse shows available—from small "saddle club" affairs to the Quarter Horse Congress—presents almost any level of competitive effort. Even in areas of substantial professional preeminence, such as cutting, sponsoring organizations have wisely taken great care to provide for vigorous amateur participation and schedule graduated events for people and horses of differing experience and ability.

When thinking about a possible show-ring "debut," the first considerations are what kind of a show to go to and, no less important, what attitude toward it you should adopt. Even if you're entering just for "fun," your approach can't be casual. Why? Because success can't be attained except by pretty rigorous preparation, and because you won't derive satisfaction from the experience unless you go at it in an organized, methodical way.

Some people go to their first horse show like somebody trying Mexican cooking for the first time; they want to take a little taste and decide if they like it. If that's your attitude, then make sure you "try" a good horse show first or you won't get a decent taste of what it's like. What is a good horse show? It needn't be large or prestigious, but it ought to be well organized, have a diversity of classes, a reputation for looking after the interests and comforts of exhibitors—and provide adequate judging. I have long been convinced that if you have a really nice young "green" horse, the easiest place to get him beaten by mediocre stock is in some small, badly managed "punkin" show, principally because you're apt to run into some really weird judging. I think this conclusion holds true, too, for a serious-minded person anxious to go into horse showing. There is a belief that small, out-of-the-way shows are good places to get "experience." That may be true, but not all the experience is the kind you'd want. It's better, even for the novice, to get "skunked" in a good class than to place or even win in a class that doesn't even approach a fair competitive level. The bigger show, too, has sufficient variety to allow you to find a class or classes matching you and your horse's stage of training. There is something to be said for "sanctioned" shows, those staged under the authority and rules of the breed associations (Quarter Horse, Appaloosa, Arabian, and others), assuming you own a registered animal.

There are a good number of first-rate "half-breds" around.[1] I've sat on a few grade horses that were as good as anything that ever wore a bridle. But if I were going out to buy a horse for showing, I'd buy a registered horse, not that there is a guarantee that he'd be better, only that owning him would allow me to compete in shows sponsored by breed associations. On the whole, these shows are more attractive than the "open" kind, particularly in regard to the more careful licensing of the judges employed. Nothing can discourage the novice more than to attain a substantial level of skill, thoroughly prepare, execute well in the show ring, and then run into erratic, ignorant judging. It's discouraging and, most of the time, unnecessary.

At the same time, you ought to have reasonable, realistic expectations. How many times have I seen horse dealers tout a customer by promising instant, overnight success in the ring, regardless of the ineptitude of the customer, if only he would dig out his fountain pen and buy the horse? But how many times, too, have I watched the predictable despair of the new owner after his first times out in the ring? You can't expect to corral the silverware the first time out. Experience, exposure, are inescapable prerequisites for success; riding in the show ring demands a knowledge of ring tactics, as well as riding ability and a good horse. It is, after all, a public performance and it takes some experience.

Horse owners are understandably proud of their animals. What other decent attitude would a horseman take? On the other hand, you have to be realistic. Not every horse, despite its merits,

[1]These days, the term half-bred has come to mean virtually any horse except one carrying registration papers in one of the recognized breeds. The great majority of horses, currently, can claim one registered parent anyway, as the nature of horse breeding stresses breed identification far more than it used to. With most horses now bred for pleasure or recreation, few of the good old "cold bloods" seen on ranches and, in days past, in the army exist anymore.

belongs in the show ring, even in "fun" shows. Happily, well-conceived western horse shows offer such a spread of events (equitation, pleasure, trail, reining, and so on) that there is usually something for everybody. But there is a question of attitude. Even if horse showing is for fun, it is a public competition, and competition of any kind requires a "winning" attitude. I have told students for years that one rides into the ring with the intention of "winning it all." I don't think there's an alternative point of view.

But you have to have the means of winning in order to legitimately entertain that attitude. You, as the rider, must have the skill to win, you must have made the pre-show preparations that are necessary, and you must have the horse that can do the job. If you think, now, that I'm making a pitch for the indispensability of high-priced show horses, keep these thoughts in mind: (1) you can win in the show ring on modestly priced horses *if* you can train and prepare them adequately; (2) your skill can go a long way in compensating for the shortcomings of the horse; (3) you can find respectable competitive situations, if you look for them, that tally with the quality of your horse. But you must realize that there are certain qualitative minimums that you must sensibly recognize. You might have a heck of a trail horse in your barn, but perhaps he just doesn't move well enough on the rail to justify sticking him in the show ring. Also, there are fashions, fads, in the show ring (many of them quite illogical) that may affect your success, although this is less true, thank goodness, of western horses on the whole.

Let's face it, showing costs some loot. Even packing up "Old Bones" into a trailer and hauling him down the road for an afternoon costs money. Granted that showing horses, at least on a local level, is hardly an extravagant hobby, any expenditure ought to be rationally justified—and some otherwise useful horses just won't pay the freight, figuratively speaking, at the horse show. And the psychological prospect for the owner is like banging your head against a wall; in the end it's futile.

What I'm saying is that showing horses ought to be fun, but that doesn't mean that it can be done without work, dedication, and even sacrifice, perhaps. There's no law on the books that says you have to show horses, although frequently there's a good deal of "social" pressure on owners of good horses to show them even if the owners, for one reason or another, aren't disposed to do so. But if you elect to join the game, go all out and play to win.

The Pleasure Class as the First Experience

Most youngsters begin their show careers in *equitation* classes (horsemanship rather than the horse to be judged). This is reasonable, although most juniors also choose to show in other events, right off the bat. At times there are equitation classes for adults, but I've never been too enthusiastic about these. In most cases, the logical show debut for adults involves signing up for the *amateur western pleasure* class. It is the most reasonable class to start with because, in one sense, the demands made on the exhibitor are simple: he has only to walk, jog, and lope his horse in both directions of the ring, line up and back. That is reason enough for this to be your first ring experience. But the simplicity is deceptive. Because the demands made on the horses in pleasure classes are not too strenuous (contrasted with performance classes like reining), almost any horse that is alive can lumber around the ring at the three gaits. Consequently, pleasure classes are usually large and they are often decided by very fine gradations of quality that not only stress the ability of the horse but also the finesse of the rider. It *looks* easy, but in fact it is a surprisingly tricky class to ride. From long observation, I believe that winning a first-rate pleasure class calls for more disciplined skill than many of the more flamboyant events.

I don't say this to be discouraging—the pleasure class *is* the place to commence your experience as a show rider—but you should be aware from the start of the competitive difficulties. It is a class in which those awful public disasters that you conjure up in your imagination (like falling off, going off course, or losing control of the horse) are reassuringly unlikely. But it is also a class in which winning is a matter involving skill and even a certain amount of luck.

The Pleasure Horse

You start, of course, with a "pleasure horse." Presumably the class is to be judged on the basis of the "pleasure" to the rider that the horse appears to provide: he should be obedient, calm, smooth-gaited, and attractive to look at. These are mere generalities that only open the door to discussion, though, about what is a pleasure horse. "Pleasure" is a subjective criterion—even in the minds of a judge conscious of the rule book or the class descriptions he's working from. Conceptions of western pleasure horses, among various breeds, range from flashy, "bridle-path hacks" exhibited under stock saddles to especially well-gaited stock horse types. Getting down to cases, the considerations listed below ought to guide you in estimating your own horse's potential success as a pleasure horse or in helping you in buying one.

(1) The horse must have faultless manners. This may even mean that the horse is a trifle phlegmatic, lacks the quickness, the athletic aptitude of a stock horse, although a good pleasure horse can't be downright "doggy," either. Pleasure classes are often really large—thirty or forty entries are not uncommon—and in the middle of one you have the feeling of being in a slow-paced cavalry charge. The horse under you must be unflappable.

(2) Gaits are essentially the real means of sorting out pleasure horses. The walk must be free, elastic, low, and executed with some speed. The jog, while relaxed, must be short, cadenced, with haunches slightly engaged, and slow. Occasionally these days pleasure horses are asked to extend at the trot, to "trot out," but a horse showing a well-cadenced jog usually has no trouble with this if given a little practice at it.[2] The lope must be similarly relaxed, low-moving, balanced, and slow.

Notice the repetition of the word "slow." That is the key to the present pleasure class. The jog and lope must be slowed to the point of risking breaking gait (more about this later). The good pleasure horse should be able to lope "for ten minutes under the shade of one tree." The precision of gait transitions is vital.

(3) The head carriage or "set" in pleasure horses is much argued about these days, the extremes going from the bent-over, stiff, wrongly collected horses that are blatant travesties of the so-called "California style" to the low-headed, stiff horses whose

[2] The reason why a western pleasure horse is asked to extend at the trot baffles me. There are times when a western horse might be asked to trot along, coming out of that pleasant jog into what is really an "ordinary" trot. But such occasions, like checking fence or trotting behind a truck, are strictly utilitarian (and not too frequent) and I don't see what the ordinary trot (for which western gear was not designed anyway) has to do with pleasure riding.

front ends look like ironing boards. The head carriage of the pleasure horse ought to be generally similar to that of the stock horse: fairly low, with bend at the throat latch, the jaw relaxed with no signs of rein tension.

(4) Unfortunately, not all ring pleasure horses have as soft mouths as the "loose rein" specification in the rule books. But the pleasure horse ought to be highly responsive to the hand aids where the most minute pressure gets results. The rein must "float," so that the horse's willingness to flex, to "back down" at the jog, and to lope should be given without severe bit restraint.

(5) The pleasure horse need not have a "quick" rein (although some excellent pleasure horses also show in western riding, "medal" type equitation classes, and even reining). But he should have the appearance of handiness. He is not asked to do a "quick stop," but he should come off the lope promptly, slightly sliding behind.

(6) Conformation *does* play an important part in pleasure-horse competition, despite the coy language about "appropriateness." The pleasure horse has to have looks. What kind? Many of the breeds more or less accept the Quarter Horse standards. Exceptions include the Arabian and the Morgan. But in any case, the pleasure horse should be a good representative of the breed, and a bit of refinement doesn't hurt, either. Some show people think it's helpful to have a flashy horse for pleasure classes (e.g., a sorrel with white socks or a gray) that can be picked out of a crowd.

Show Tack

The tack used for pleasure classes (and also for trail and equitation classes) has become pretty well standardized these days, not by rules but by custom. The "show" saddle is one that displays a discreet amount of silver trim. The use of silver ornamentation on saddles in the show ring is of fairly long standing, but fashions ebb and flow regarding how much is preferred. We have just passed through a time in which show saddles almost came to resemble those "silver-mounted" parade saddles still actually to be seen in street parades. The current trend is to less silver. The trim is a matter of preference, but such adornments as silver conchos, horn caps, cantle plates and plates on the rear skirting, and medallions on the stirrups are conventional. Most show saddles have rolled bindings on the Cheyenne roll and gullet, usually silver-laced. Aesthetically speaking, I have always considered the carving on the leather more an enhancement to the saddle than silver, and there is an unfortunate tendency at the moment to try to dress up mediocre saddles with silver embellishments. Show saddles not custom-made tend, for some reason, to be built on trees one would not select for an ordinary working saddle. The use of built-up foam-rubber seats are unfortunately common in ready-made show saddles. Try to find a show saddle, if you need and want one, similar in basic design to the saddle you use every day—and don't save the show rig just for the ring. Ride in it frequently so you're thoroughly accustomed to it.

The amount and quality of the silver informally required depends, to some degree, on what breed you're showing. The Arabians, for example, go in for elaborate silver, with the Quarter Horse people only just behind. Other breeds tend to be less fussy, some of them even encouraging the use of good working rigs naked of silver trim. The matter of bits is illustrative. A good silver-mounted bit ranges from one hundred dollars upwards. Silver bits are virtually a requirement for showing Arabians, but plain bits of excellent quality are often seen in other shows.

The show saddle is set either on a first-quality blanket, preferably a Navaho, or on a soft, synthetic pad, colored or white. Hair and quilted pads are not used. The choice depends on your taste; if you are more traditional you'll lean toward the blanket. Coronas under the saddle have been out of style for years and now even the heavy fringing on saddle blankets, once favored, is frowned on.

It is customary in pleasure and trail classes to carry a small *reata* of braided leather or hair on the rope hanger, but not a full-sized lariat. This is a useless appendage (a real honest-to-goodness rope would make more sense), but it is the style. It is also the style to carry braided leather hobbles either on the back cinch (if one is used in the ring) or attached by saddle strings behind the cantle. Comparatively few horses are hobble-broke these days and this is a non-functional item. Breast collars have suddenly made a reappearance in the show ring, invariably narrow ones often with silver embellishment. They really serve no purpose under show conditions, but fashion rarely obeys logic.

Show bridles come in two basic types: one-ear and the browband type with a throat latch. They are almost always silver-mounted. The reins, too, are usually lightly trimmed with silver, often ferrules. In California and Arizona, the *romal* is close to being universal and it is beginning to appear farther east.[3] Elsewhere, split reins are the custom. Bits are usually silver-worked or mounted, ranging from "cowboy" snaffles to Half-Breeds and Spades, the latter popular in California. These Spanish-type bits were originally used with rein chains, but these are not seen anymore. Rules now permit the use of conventional curb chains as well as straps.

For a time it was popular to discard the back cinch in pleasure classes, some show rigs even constructed with single-rigging. This practice seems to be passing and double-rigging is more common (as I think it ought to be). Sheepskin or synthetic-material cinch covers are often seen in the ring, and these are useful items under most conditions.

Getting Dressed for the Show Ring

The rider's dress is an integral part of the turnout. Some aspects of your attire are determined by rules common to most shows, some are matters of custom. There is actually little difference between male and female outfits, except in terms of color and, more recently, the popularity of women's "saddle suits" (matching pants, vests, and shirts).

A hat is always worn, of course. The practice of wearing hats in bright reds, yellows, pastel greens, and wines by women is questionable to my tastes, but in any event the impulse for matching items can be taken too far; it is a bit overdone to have

---

[3]The *romal* is essentially a pair of reins that come together at the end to form a quirt (although contemporary *romals* usually have only a double thickness of leather at the end). The quirt or doubled end is attached to the reins as they come together by a metal "D" or a swivel. The *romal* is held differently from split reins (the reins coming up through the hand from the bottom) and, in my view, it is a far less delicate piece of equipment, at least when used on horses not trained in the classic California method.

135

hat, shirt, pants, even chaps, all matching. The costume of a rodeo queen and a show rider are not identical.

Shirts must be long-sleeved and worn with a tie (of a wide range of types, from "chokers" to flowing scarf ties). Jackets of "western" cut and trim are suitable if the weather requires, but pass up leather ones with yards of fringe attached. Vests are coming back into popularity and they are a real practical piece of gear.

Boots are necessary and I think that spurs ought to be worn on them, although that's optional in most rule books. Some people have a pair of extra fancy spurs they save for shows.

Chaps are almost universally required. The "shotgun" style dominates in the show ring, but I would like to see a revival of the "batwing" in the ring, too. The batwing chap is immensely comfortable. Chaps can be too gaudy; some of them look as if they came out of a science-fiction movie.

Most people wear gloves and I think you get a better feel on the reins with them. A tip to the ladies: make sure your hair is well done up under your hat and that the hat fits. There is nothing more disconcerting than losing your hat and having your hairdo fall down (or so they tell me). Wear a western hat well down on the forehead, not toward the back of the head like a bonnet. I think there's something incongruous about earrings under a western hat, but that doesn't bother a lot of people. I'd be inclined to say that you ought to express your fondness for jewelry by collecting trophy buckles.

Take some care with your turnout. Nobody looks scruffy anymore in the show ring. It's not a fashion show, but attention to small details of tack and clothing is a factor in the judge's overall impression.

The Appearance of the Horse

Needless to say, the horse ought to enter the ring in immaculate condition. Quarter Horse exhibitors and those who follow their lead now show horses with short, *pulled* manes. These manes must be manually "pulled" with a pulling comb to a length of about three to four inches. The mane should, of course, be thinned in the process. The forelock is also carefully pulled. The mane is roached (clipped with electric clippers) from just behind the poll down the neck or crest about one quarter of the distance to the withers or less. This has been called the "bridle path," and clipping here was originally designed to allow the crown piece of the bridle to rest smoothly on the upper part of the neck. Nowadays, the tendency has been to trim much farther down the crest. This is a matter of taste again, but I would prefer trimming the western horse like the hunter, leaving the mane up to within only three or four inches of the poll and forelock (just enough to clear the way for the crown piece). This is not the current style, but, as more Quarter Horses do double duty in the ring as hunters as well as stock horses, this style may become more widespread.[4] In any case, don't get careless with the clippers and take off too much mane. Tails are pulled, too. In the old days, the tails of Quarter Horses were drastically shortened, but now the length is similar to that traditional for hunters and cavalry horses; the tail is pulled so that, at rest, it falls at or slightly below the point of the hock. Arabians, Morgans, and some other breeds show western horses with full, unpulled manes and long tails.

The horse need not be body-clipped, but should be clipped on the legs (below the knee) and the head. Most show horses have their ears clipped. This may be an arguable practice in that the hairs in the ears offer some protection against flies and dirt. Trimmed ears do greatly enhance the appearance of the head, though, and it may be worthwhile if the horse is barn-maintained.

Hoofs should be blackened (there are a number of commercial products for this purpose) if the hoof wall is dark, and if the hoof wall is light-colored, covered with a clear preparation (also commercially available). If the horse has only one light hoof, it is usual to blacken all of them.

Preparations for the Ring

It is often said that success in showing is "seventy-five percent stable management." There is a good deal of truth in that, especially in terms of fitness and conditioning. Even for pleasure classes, the horse must be fit. This simply means miles of work.

[4]Not so many years ago, Quarter Horses were shown with completely roached manes (like roping horses are still trimmed). The advent of quarter-horse racing ushered in the new mane style that resembles the way manes of Thoroughbreds are kept.

Make certain the diet is not just adequate, but that it contributes to keeping the coat in top condition. Most professionals like to augment the basic ration of show horses with supplements designed to enhance the appearance of the coat. This can be done by adding linseed meal to the feed or adding a handful of Calf Manna to the grain ration.

We cannot go into the subject of training here, but we can discuss the problems of getting the novice rider ready. His essential need is to recreate, as far as possible, the conditions of the show ring. Assuming that you're working with a "made" horse, a horse ready to take you into your first pleasure class, there are a number of ways to help *you* prepare. Preparation for the show ring is a little like getting ready for a battle; the key idea is *repetition*, so that habit becomes a more powerful influence than anxiety or mental confusion.

The basic technique, not unlike producing a play, is *rehearsal*. For some classes, like reining, exact rehearsal may not be desirable, but for pleasure classes there is no harm and many advantages in more or less exactly reproducing the conditions of the ring. This rehearsal approach subdivides into three main areas of attention: (1) ring procedures; (2) gait transitions and "backing down"; (3) ring tactics.

(1) It is simple to reproduce ring procedures in your own practice ring. You can even let your imagination have full play. I have occasionally put a portable radio next to the rail, had people stand against the ring fence, and tied flags and pennants to the fence. Get your friends and fellow students to ride with you if possible, to make up a facsimile class. A volunteer on foot can "play" ringmaster and judge.

Start at the beginning. Enter the ring and track left at a walk. Have someone give the announcer's commands, like "Jog, please," or "Walk, walk your horses, please." In a pleasure class the horses are walked, then jogged, then returned to the walk, then loped, then walked and reversed, the three main gaits repeated in the opposite direction. Then the horses are called to line up across the ring. Have the volunteer on foot walk up to you, examine your horse, and ask you to back three steps. Keep in mind that your number may be called again and you'll return to the rail to work again. I have even had students practice responding to the announcement of the placings of the class and riding up to receive a ribbon. There is nothing like optimism.

(2) Practice "on the rail" with a special emphasis on gait transitions. The pleasure horse should respond to commands for change of gait rapidly but with an easy composure. These transitions are crucial. The horse should slip smoothly into the jog without it being necessary to rein him back to shorten stride after a diagonal or two. The motion into the lope should be immediate and precise without any appearance of bounding into the slow gallop. The horse should always leave into the lope *straight* on the track. The downward transitions should be instantaneous without being abrupt, the horse shortening without the appearance of undue restraint. The transition from lope to walk must be relatively quick, the horse suggesting a half-stop with a noticeable engagement of the haunches, even a mild sliding effect.

While working the rail at jog and lope, you should practice "backing down." By this I mean the process of tactfully even unnoticeably, slowing the horse, shortening the stride. Right or wrong, pleasure classes are won and lost on the basis of the slowness of these gaits, and you must practice the subtle art of encouraging the horse to keep to his gait while reducing his progress to the slowest possible execution of the gait short of breaking the stride. This entails the gentlest of hand aids, nicely balanced with leg support. Squeezing ever so delicately with the fingers on what must be a floating rein, the horse "backs down" for you, while you preserve his impulsion, his engagement, by harmonious support from the legs. Sometimes even the slightest pressure from the lower legs may be too much, and this is the one time when knee pressure may be called for since its mild effect will only tend to confirm your desire for the horse to maintain the gait.

It takes practice to bring the hand and leg aids into this fine balance, and the "backing down" technique is really only applicable to riding pleasure classes. By practice you'll be able to sense what the horse is doing underneath you, what is, in fact, the limit of his ability to slow the pace and shorten the stride. Ideally, when the horse is traveling right, you should have the sensation that he is just about to break gait—come off the jog into the walk, for example—but he doesn't. Many novices don't realize, at first, just how slow a good pleasure horse can move, properly ridden. That takes the experience of riding a few pretty sharp horses. Keep in mind while practicing backing down that evenness of gait is still imperative. The judge should not be aware that you're backing down, it's that subtle. Backing down is not a transition at all, as, for example, moving from a slow to an ordinary lope would be. It is a slight contraction of stride within a given variation of gait and it should be attained as quickly as feasible, allowing the rider to carefully maintain the stride he's managed to set.

(3) I'll go into the more specific aspects of ring tactics in a moment, but here I want to stress the usefulness of ring practice with the addition of other riders. Once again you'll have to press your friends into service. You must get accustomed to having horses around you at close quarters. In the show ring they'll be next to you, in front of you, and behind you. What do you do when you have to lope with a horse on the rail just in front of you? When should you pass another horse? What happens when an over-eager horse gallops up on your heels? How should you handle yourself if you get into a jam on the corners?

I'll try to answer some of these questions later on, but these problems have a way of seriously disconcerting inexperienced riders and the best way to start learning to cope is to "rehearse" with a few other riders in the ring. In the instructional situation, I have frequently had a couple of well-trained show riders actually reproduce some sticky situations for the novice who's getting ready for his baptism in the show ring, just to give him a taste of what sort of predicaments he might encounter. Other things being equal, it would be desirable if you could make your debut in a small class of eight or ten, but that isn't too likely and you might as well prepare yourself for a class of twenty or even more.

Before You Face the Ring

Something ought to be said about pre-class preparations at the show grounds themselves. The atmosphere of the horse show, its physical setting, can be rather intimidating the first time you're in the midst of it as a participant. The beginner is understandably nervous, like having "opening-night" jitters. Everyone he sees seems more accustomed to it all than he is. The horses he spots look magnificent, unbeatable. Above all, the place is like a madhouse, people rushing around, yelling, horses, trailers, and vans milling together, the public-address system issuing ominous and often inexplicable directions.

The best insurance against pre-show anxiety is not to get flustered, and the best way to accomplish that is not to be in a hurry. Get there early so that you have plenty of time. Finish up all the official rituals (picking up numbers, confirming classes, and so on) early so you can concentrate on the horse. A good slice of time must be set aside for the final grooming session, and that is a fine way to keep busy and to forget about your nervousness. As a general rule, plan to tack up the horse about forty-five minutes before your class is to get its final call. You'll want a half hour in the warm-up ring and fifteen minutes afterward so that you can get off the horse, relax, and prepare yourself mentally for the class.

The warm-up ring contains all the pressures of the whole show magnified. It is a place where some people get "psyched out." The warm-up ring is usually filled with a mob of riders, some of whom are downright egocentric at best, rude at worst. Not only is there confusion, but to the novice everyone seems ruthlessly bent on harrassing him. This isn't true, it only seems so. You must try to preserve your cool by paying strict attention to your own horse and what *you* are doing. Forget about the other fellow, except to avoid collisions. You will see people in warm-up rings doing all sorts of weird things, but just because you're not doing them doesn't mean you've neglected some vital preparation. As a matter of fact, it is wise to take it easy in the warm-up ring. All you want to do is "uncork" your horse a little, let him get his joints moving, and this means you'll likely be walking and jogging him, with a short period at the lope. Just because riders around you are dashing here and there, doing quick stops, figure eights, or even whacking their beasts with crops doesn't mean that you're not doing what you ought to be doing. Take it easy and first *warm up*. That's what you're there for.

Finally, the Show Ring: Tactics

The main tactic in a pleasure-horse class is to create the illusion of a thoroughly pleasurable conveyance. I use the word "illusion" because, candidly, not all good show-ring pleasure horses are, without very skilled presentation, pure pleasures to sit on. The word "illusion" also tends to emphasize the fact that pleasure classes are won or lost (beyond the matter of training preparation) on showmanship, that elusive but vital ingredient that makes classes of this sort distinctly different from performance classes. The pleasure class is a sort of mini-drama in which the participants are engaged in creating a short, intense visual impression. From the judge's perspective, the class is a kaleidoscope of moving images, some of which arrest his attention and some that don't. Even with the most businesslike and experienced judges, small, even trifling elements affect his judgment, visual images that register on his mind, though he himself may be totally unaware of their impact. The contestant, then, is in the business of creating those impressive, favorable images—and that, in a real sense, is showmanship.

One of the principal problems in showing in pleasure classes is their sheer size. It is easy to get lost in the crowd. Unfortunately, you can't just tuck in next to the rail and "do your thing." Being a part of this moving cavalcade, "positioning" becomes of extreme importance—where you are in relationship to the rest of the class. And because the emphasis in western pleasure is on slowness at the jog and lope, it is difficult to maneuver in and out of undesirable positions without tampering with the evenness of your pace. This means that gaining position at the walk is all that more significant. You don't want to be masked from the judge's view by a screen of competitors. There are advantages to working against the rail, but you can also get lost on the rail, hidden behind a troop of other horses. If you choose to stay on the rail, make sure that when you enter the ring at the walk you position yourself so that you are not cut off from view when the jog is called for. Even though you may have thought you picked an open spot on the rail with ample interval, other horses may move in on you and you must be prepared to reposition.

The walk is more important than most exhibitors believe. The first appearance you want to create is one of composure and relaxation, but with the horse walking ahead briskly. You must encourage this impulsion at the walk by subtle, imperceptible leg aids. Make the horse walk out. At the walk you may have your only opportunity to pass other contestants, to change position by increasing speed. Remember you are only being judged when actually observed. Needless to say, you can't play cat-and-mouse with the judge, but you should be conscious of his approximate location in the ring and you can certainly steal a sideways glance at him now and again. During this initial period at the walk, you can also change positioning by halting or circling if you determine that the judge is otherwise occupied. There is no rule against halting or circling, by the way, but it is prudent to do so when the judge is not looking directly at you.

Even though the pleasure class demands concentration and tactical keeness, the impression you should produce is one of serene confidence. You should not look as if you're working hard or very conscious of the competition. You're showing a horse, of course, and you should ride as if you knew your mount was the best and all you had to do was to let him perform. You should be all business, but appear casual, in other words. This impression of ease can be conveyed at the walk—and first impressions are often decisive.

When the call comes for the jog, don't rush it. Respond with reasonable promptness, but this transition is very important and should not be hurried. After all, at the jog and lope the more people who pass you the better. The trick in making this transition is to slip into the jog without occasioning the need to shorten stride after the slow trot has been attained. But if you must apply some rein tension at this point, during the first couple of trot diagonals, try to do it without seeming to take back the rein. The way to ride the jog in the show ring is to "back down" to where you feel that the horse is about to break gait and come to the walk. No horse will jog that slow on a wholly loose rein. You must have some contact; you must hold him together. Also, only by some leg pressure will you create enough impulsion to stay on the jog; the legs should keep him well on the bit. The aids, as we've said so often before, must be delicately balanced and also inconspicuous.

Appear oblivious to all around you, but, in fact, keep very alert. This is particularly necessary when you come to the lope. It is crucial that you pre-position yourself prior to the call for the lope. Avoid circling if you can, but try to get some daylight, preferably on the rail. You don't want a horse in front of you or next to you. And if you've already made some "mental notes" about your competitors, identifying some of them as unsteady and likely to get "nervy" at the lope, you don't want a horse of that sort on your heels going into the lope.

Get the horse away into the lope crisply, steadying him up a

The pleasure horse at the slow lope. The lope of the pleasure horse is slow and relaxed, creating an impression of comfort and economy of movement. Here, the horse is a trifle "strung out" at the lope; the rider is sitting a bit behind the balance of the horse.

little if necessary. Let other horses pass you, but try to avoid the need to pass anyone else. If your horse seems eager, it's not a bad idea to tuck him in behind a slow-moving, deliberate horse and let your competition run interference for you. There are three main considerations in showing at the lope: (1) getting away evenly; (2) not getting hidden away in the crowd; (3) avoiding an acceleration of pace as you're being passed by other horses. If you can remain on the rail and accomplish these objectives, stay there. But frequently you'll have to come off the rail toward the center of the ring. Judges, as a rule, dislike exhibitors sharply cutting corners, appearing to hog the limelight by coming too far into the center of the arena. Don't appear to be trying to get between the judge and the rest of the class. The corners, too, are places where you're apt to be uneven. Horses usually need to be attentively ridden in the corners as they tend either to want to hurry or, quite the opposite, fall off the bit and get "doggy."

Ride defensively. Occasionally you'll run up against an exhibitor who will actually weave through a class like an ambulance on the way to an accident. It would be handy to have eyes with 360-degree vision. But since you don't, the next best choice is to try, out of the corners of your eyes, to keep a watch on the competition so you'll have some warning of what they're likely to do. After you ride a few classes, you'll be surprised at how quickly and easily you can "catalogue" the other horses and riders in a class, you'll have a fair idea of what to expect, in both behavior and performance. Of course, it's also a good practice to have some notion of where the judge is situated in the ring. Judges know that exhibitors try to determine where they are and so they often move around the arena, trying to see the class from a number of angles and keep the exhibitors guessing. It is certainly true that a judge can only judge what he sees—and this means that some mistakes are missed—but you can't appear to be watching the judge all the time. Occasionally, though, you can see him without twisting your head around and discover that he's looking away from you; this *is* the time for needed adjustments, if any. But if you are caught in an error—the most common is a wrong lead—correct yourself immediately. Don't imagine the judge isn't going to recognize the mistake.

At all three gaits, try to give the impression that it's all really a pleasure. This doesn't mean anything theatrical (in which I include smiling fondly at the judge as you ride past). Just be cool.

When the horses have been worked both ways, you'll be asked to come in and line up. Respond, but don't be in a hurry. There's an advantage to not being among the first to line up, but you shouldn't look as if you're holding back from coming in, either. In general, avoid the extreme ends of the lineup if you can, and try not to get sandwiched too closely between horses. Stand the horse squarely on his legs, reins limp but not thrown away. Don't slouch in the saddle but don't sit in a stiff brace, either. This is a pleasure class, not a review of the household cavalry. When asked to back, do it briskly with as little cueing as you can get away with. Three or four steps are sufficient and then come back on line. It is better to back straight and with a minimum of force than to emphasize quickness. The judge may well circle your horse, inspecting it. Look to the front and if he speaks to you (unlikely but possible) you may turn to face him in order to answer his question or comment *briefly*.

In large pleasure-horse classes, it is common to excuse a part of the class after the initial work and request the remaining exhibitors to work again. Or the judge may hold some horses in the center of the ring and work a selected number again on the rail. Remember your number so that you can respond to instructions. Also, if you are confused over which group you belong to, address your inquiry to the ringmaster (or "ring steward"), not the judge. It is considered poor form for an exhibitor to speak directly to the judge in the ring unless the judge initiates the conversation. Don't second-guess the judge as to the meaning of his division of the class. Judges work differently and you can't be absolutely certain of the final "tieing" of the class until the results are announced. I'll remember as long as I live the expression on the face of a young girl in the pleasure class I once judged. She was the one outstanding exhibitor in what was otherwise a mediocre class. My problem was how to select second and third places and so on. So I asked a number of horses to work again, but I saw no purpose in looking at the winner a second time. When this girl was not called out to work again, her face was a remarkable combination of disbelief and melancholy. She brightened up considerably, though, when the results were announced. She was so surprised she almost fell out of the saddle. Moral? Don't count yourself out until the results are given over the P.A. system.

"Psyching" judges is an old game: trying to figure out what a

The line-up. The suspense builds as the judge moves down the row of exhibitors. This is the final act of the mini-drama of a horse-show class.

given judge is looking for. Let me make three very brief observations about this: (1) judging is, within limits, a subjective evaluation, a matter of the individual tastes of the judge. Good judging is, in consequence, consistent judging. You may not agree with the judge's tastes, but if he maintains a consistent standard it indicates that he has a clear, theoretically cogent notion of what he likes. (2) Don't try to radically modify how you show your horse to presumably suit some particular judge on some particular day. Do what you do well and stick to it. Winning in the show ring is a matter of taking advantage of the law of averages, and what one judge prefers another doesn't; in the long run you'll get your share of the silverware by being yourself, consistent. (3) It is perfectly permissible to go up to the judge *after the show* and solicit his opinion or ask for a more extended evaluation. He is not officially obliged to give it, but most judges are cooperative about this and anxious to help and explain. You can obviously learn something from judges. On the other hand, keep in mind that what you will be receiving is opinion, which must be weighed in your mind against other factors, other opinions.

Horse showing is a little like horse racing. What happens in one class (or one race) may not repeat itself in another. In showing pleasure horses, factors of horse quality aside, the main element in winning is the avoidance of mistakes. In a good pleasure class, one obvious mistake is enough to eliminate you from consideration (errors like a wrong lead, a bad gait transition, or a minor disobedience). But the *less* obvious mistakes must be avoided, too, in order to create the visual impression, already discussed, that leads to blue ribbons. The beginner in the show ring is bound to make some mistakes, hopefully the less obvious kinds, but inexperience, stage fright, and the ordinary mental lapses that affect us all will have to be overcome. Every class is a fresh start, but every completed class is a source of insight. Try to analyze these classes with an eye to recognizing what you did well and less well. The concentration of ring riding often has a peculiar way of blocking out recall of details. For this reason, if you have a knowledgeable friend, it's intelligent to get an on-the-ground critique, too.

Horse showing is sport. Ride to win, but don't lose your sense of proportion. If you do, it will stop being fun. Winning is very gratifying, but it is not the primary gratification. That is an inner satisfaction that silver trophies only enhance but cannot replace.

8

The Ultimate Art—
Riding the Stock Horse

There may be some debate about what's the "ultimate art" in western horsemanship. In the last chapter we spent some time discussing the riding of pleasure horses, and that's no mean art. I suppose every phase of a very diversified form of equestrian sport has its advocates, those who plump for their speciality as the "ultimate art."[1] But the western horse is fundamentally a stock horse, as I've tried to argue elsewhere in the book, and in stock work—in a sense the most practically grounded of all phases of western horsemanship—I believe the levels of horse management reach their highest expression. As you may remember, I've used the term "stock horse" broadly, but now I want to be more specific in usage and talk about the riding of horses that actually work cattle or, to put it more technically, "reined cow horses"

[1] Have you ever gone to a dog show? What's remarkable about them is that there are enthusiastic fanciers of nearly every known canine form, even the most grotesque and absurd. "Function" clearly means different things to different people. This is true of horses, too. The two forms of horses that are to me the least attractive are American Saddlebred five-gaited horses and Arabian "Park" horses, although I have nothing against Saddlebreds or Arabians as a breed. Yet I know of people who go into fits of ecstasy over these specialties and consider the riding of them to be true art.

and "cutting horses." The roping horse works cattle, too, and is entitled to the designation, "stock horse," but the roping horse is a participant in a very specialized event and he is trained accordingly to very demanding specialized standards. However, the riding aspect of roping competition is secondary. This does not mean that calf ropers are not superb horsemen, only that the riding involved is of brief duration (a few seconds actually) and not extremely varied in its requirements. For this reason, I'm concentrating in this chapter on riding reined cow horses and, to a lesser extent, cutting horses by implication. The riding and training of stock horses, especially competitive cow and cutting horses, would require a separate book at the very least, even assuming that it was possible to capture the main aspects of this art on the printed page. I am trying here to introduce the whole area of stock-horse riding to the novice-turned-semi-experienced rider, someone who has, in effect, mastered the contents of this book up to this point. I suppose that you could say that having assimilated the contents of this book, the rider might go into competitive trail riding, reining, roping, even polo, but I have chosen to promote the riding of the stock horse for two reasons: (1) it is the most logical outgrowth of the principles of horseman-ship I've discussed so far; (2) I have a personal bias in favor of the stock horse as the ultimate expression of western horsemanship. The last point is not to be taken as holy writ, only as a private advocacy.

Cattle Make the Difference

Stock-horse riding involves working the horse on cattle—and this factor radically changes the game. It introduces the element of another animal and its behavior, forcing upon both rider and horse a further dimension of tactics and a test of harmonious horsemanship. The moves that horse and rider make are in reply, chiefly, to those made by the cow, demanding an extraordinary new sensitivity on the part of the rider and often a new initiative on the part of the horse (especially in cutting).

Reduced to the competitive game (either cow-horse classes or cutting competition), the aim is the control of cattle under circumstances in which the cow has a natural inclination to resist such control. Success at it depends not only on the rigorous training of the horse and intimate cooperation between horse and rider, but also both horse's and rider's knowledge of cattle. This is a new dimension, but it cannot be overlooked. These days it is not unusual at all for a good horseman to take up riding cutting horses or stock horses without much, if any, experience with cattle. This means, at base, that the novice must learn the game at the same time he's learning something about cattle and their behavior. Obviously, a top reining horse, worked only on "dry" patterns, must learn about cows if he's going to become a reined cow horse. There must be a tempering of that instinct that we call "cow" or "cow sense."

Cattle are not like horses. Their mental processes are very different. Those telltale signs that horsemen come to respond to in horses (position of the ears, tail movements, and so on) aren't applicable to cattle. Indeed, an experienced horseman has a "sixth sense" that enables him to tell what a horse is going to do; a real cattleman has a somewhat similar instinct when it comes to cows, but the signs and the feel are different.

It may sound discouraging, but I don't think a person can become a polished stock-horse rider without a great deal of cattle know-how. The problem is how to get it, unless you live on a cattle ranch. However, most horse facilities that specialize in stock horses keep cattle, and that is where most novices acquire their experience and knowledge. It may sound strange, but a good way to learn about cattle is to work with and around them on foot. There's nothing like being really close to what you're trying to study. I knew an Angus rancher up in the north who rarely used horses at all, but he was a wonder at moving and sorting cattle on foot with the aid of a walking stick. Cattle, by the way, are far from stupid, and a surprising amount of "training" of them is possible if you take the time (which few people do, considering the end for which most cows are destined, I suppose). Indeed, cattle learn what cutting is all about so fast that they become quite useless for training purposes after a couple of months and you have to switch to fresh stock.

A knowledge of cattle is a rather intangible thing. It would be hard to write some sort of a guidebook on how to recognize when a cow is going to bolt, turn left or right, or duck away from you. But after a time you develop a sort of feel about what they're likely to do, and this is a great aid in stock-horse work. You can also learn to very hastily make some reasonable guesses about which cows will work best for you in competitive situations, because, of course, your selection of individual cattle to work bears on how well your "go-round" will turn out.[2]

TRAILING CATTLE

The best and quickest way to acquire a little cow sense is to trail cattle slowly. Let out a half dozen or so rather agey cows or steers into the arena. Don't use calves as they're apt to be too quick and unsettled. It's a temptation sometimes, for ease and convenience to use roping calves for stock-horse work, but on a green horse (or with a green rider) calves are inclined to move too much.

Let your small bunch of cattle close up together, as they will, keeping the horse well away from the herd, but insist that he face

Trailing the herd. The horse, calm and confident, moves behind at the proper interval, the herd bunched and unexcited. The beginning stock-horse rider must learn to "stalk" cattle like a softly moving cat. Notice the long, "floating" rein.

[2]Bovine terminology can be confusing. I have used the word "cow," as is traditional, to refer to cattle of all sexes in this general context. Of course, a "cow" is, more specifically, a female and in this sense "cows" are infrequently used in stock-horse competitions; steers (castrated males) are far more common.

it. If you're on a made cow horse, no problem, but green horses, seeing cattle for the first time, react mostly with curiosity, but sometimes also with a little apprehension. Some horses want to spin away, so leg ride the horse a bit, keeping his head toward the stock.

Don't rush things. Settle down on your horse and wait a while. Enjoy the surroundings; sit and look at the cattle for a few minutes. Let the horse do a little observing, too. After the herd is settled, often in the corner of the arena, walk the horse in behind the herd, still maybe half the arena away from it, calculating as much as possible where the cattle's heads are pointing. If the cows wheel to face you, rumps into the corner, ease the horse to the arena fence and halt, still facing the herd. The cattle may then wheel away from you and move; if they don't, creep the horse slowly along the fence, approaching the herd. If the cattle refuse to turn away from you, stop now and again and let things settle down again. Notice, if you're on a green horse, any signs of agitation on his part. If you do see that he's getting a little excited over this new activity, stop and quiet him, not moving ahead again until he's fully relaxed. As you approach, the cattle will finally turn away from you, but you don't want them to bolt, so come up to them like a bird dog starting to point a pheasant. Within fifteen to twenty feet, you can be certain that the herd will turn. The whole emphasis here is to move the cattle slowly, with as little fuss as possible. Just let them meander in front of you. Don't speak to the cattle yet, just let your presence move them. Needless to say, you don't want to slap your chaps, twirl a rope, or wave your hat à la Hollywood.

As the herd turns away from you, follow them, but still at a distance of about thirty feet or more. Chances are that the small herd will remain pretty well bunched, but it is possible, too, that there may be a "trailer" lingering behind or a cow that ranges off to the side. Don't try to head these individualists back into the herd yet by hurrying up the straggler or bringing in the outsider. Follow the main bunch slowly, keeping the horse's head down to the center of the herd. You can repeat this maneuver a number of times. It may not be particularly exciting—although I've never had a student who didn't find this early cattle work deeply fascinating—but it will give you an initial feel for working cattle the right way, and it's altogether the best way to start a horse on cattle work. After a time, you will find that the horse will follow the herd with very little, if any, cueing from your hand; in any case, you should rely mostly on your leg aids to encourage the horse's own initiative. Horses bred for cattle work show an astonishing aptitude for it. The only comparison that seems roughly similar is the hound with its instinct for trailing game.

MORE CATTLE WORK

After this first work with a small herd, the problem is to learn to trail a single cow. This is best accomplished by continuing to use a small group of cattle, but concentrating your attention and that of your horse on one selected animal. When you pick up the herd—that is, move the herd away from you as you've been practicing—choose one cow out of the group and move in closer to it, continuing to keep the pace slow. You are still walking. Speed will come later. Move with that single cow. Chances are that your "target" cow will bury itself in the middle of the herd; cows have a curious awareness of being singled out for attention. But it might, on the other hand, move to the flanks of the bunch or even briefly put a little distance between itself and the herd. If this happens, stick with that cow and you can attempt to gently turn it in, coming in behind it and on the outside. Don't, yet, try either to get too close or to press the animal. If the single cow or the small herd, for that matter, bolts, begins to run, don't pursue. Let everything settle and then begin again. If, on the other hand, your "target" cow or the herd itself merely increases speed to a jog, then let your horse jog along, too, if he remains unflustered and keeps his head down to his work. The idea is for you and the horse to learn to concentrate on trailing one animal; the horse must become conscious of being "set down" on one cow.

If, which is more likely, the cow you've selected to trail decides to bury itself in the middle of the herd, keep the horse's head "aimed" at that cow and move toward the center of the herd. The cattle will not let you crowd them, so you won't be able to actually ride in behind the target cow, but you'll get the idea across to your horse which animal you're after if you doggedly keep him headed toward that cow, toward the center of the herd if the cow chooses to remain there.

A much more ambitious undertaking involves working one cow

alone in the ring. Don't try this until the horse you're going to sit on has become very steady at the trailing work we've been discussing. If you're ready to try this, though, the single cow must be released at the end of the arena so that it will instinctively move down the arena to join the animals from which it has been separated at the opposite end, held, of course, in a pen. At this stage, you must be prepared for a little action. The cow, released from its holding pen at one end of the arena, may decide to slowly amble into the ring, mill about, look things over, and then gradually work its way to the opposite end. If this happens, merely follow it at a reasonable distance without crowding it. The purpose is to acquire experiencd trailing. Keep the horse on the target, but use as little rein effect as you can get away with, cueing with the legs. On the other hand, the cow may choose to get to the other end by a direct route—and with considerably more speed. The cow may just take off for the end. If this occurs, you must follow, increasing your horse's speed to allow you to stay with the cow. Don't, however, try to drive the cow by getting too close, and don't over-run it. If your horse is green, he may get too much into the spirit of the chase and you may need to restrain him, encouraging him to take it easy. But don't completely lose the cow. Once you're committed, stay with it.

When the cow reaches the opposite end of the arena, it will stop by the gate to the holding pen. As you approach, it may turn to face you. If it does turn to face you, stop your horse immediately. Should the cow stand relatively still facing you, begin to walk slowly toward it, closing the distance to about a dozen feet. Sooner or later, on its own initiative or because of your approach, the cow will turn left or right, trying to squeeze closer to the gate or the arena fence. As this happens, move your horse to follow the movement of the cow. The cow may duck left and right several times, probably more quickly with each movement. Keep the horse working. This will involve reining him from a virtually stationary position, using as much leg cueing as possible. If the horse resists the turns on the haunches, allow him to step forward for a step or two, but don't allow him to charge the cow. You should move with the cow only about a half-dozen times. After that, turn away and rein up. This will signal to the horse that you have finished work with this cow. Don't be tempted to swing around, then, and approach the cow along the fence and "dig him out," driving him toward the center of the arena. If you did that, the cow would duck back toward the pen gate and. at this stage, both you and the horse would be outmaneuvered. That would only be a frustrating and unfavorable experience.

WORK IN THE SMALL RING

So far we have been using a large arena, because the emphasis has been on getting familiar with cattle and trailing. Now, though, there are advantages to switching operations to a smaller ring. The ring favored by cutting-horse riders is one hundred feet square (although the circular ring is now becoming popular, due, principally, to some new techniques in cutting). You needn't be too fussy about ring sizes, but something a good deal smaller than, say, three hundred by one hundred fifty feet is necessary. The purpose of the change to a smaller arena is that now you're going to try to move cattle, to introduce control as against merely trailing.

You can let a few head into your small ring; six to ten is a reasonable number. There is also a benefit in having another rider working the ring with you, although it's not absolutely necessary. The second rider can be useful in moving and holding your herd while you're working.

The first step is to merely move the small herd for a while in the ring, trailing essentially, but in the smaller area you will be beginning to drive the stock, working closer to them. Try to keep the cattle bunched. Press them a little; those that stray out from the bunch should be turned in quickly.

After driving the cattle for a few turns around the small arena (two or three times is enough), let them settle. Your first objective is to learn to move quietly into the herd and then to divide it. Approach the herd slowly, "softly" is a good way to put it. If you are quiet and painstaking, the herd will hold its position, although there will be a considerable amount of milling around. Don't jostle them. Let your horse slip among the cattle; they will give way to you. Try first to go into the herd and stop. The individual animals in the herd will move away from you—they don't want to be rubbing against you—but chances are that the herd will remain more or less stationary, particularly if you have a "backup" or "turn-back" rider working the ring with you. Take

155

Entering the herd. You enter a herd like walking into a darkened room, almost burglar-style. Slowly and quietly, the horse moves in among the cattle without scattering them.

Splitting the herd. The horse has separated the cattle, gently moving the animals on the right of the photo. The separated group remains well bunched. The horse shows no signs of agitation, but awaits the rider's next cue.

your time. If your horse has been patiently prepared for this, he should stand quiet, alert, ready, but not jumpy. Then move toward the ring fence at the rear of the cattle. When you reach it, you have, in effect, split the herd in two. You can repeat this operation enough times so that you and the horse feel confident about entering the herd and moving to its rear.

Now you can attempt something a good deal more delicate. Enter the herd, move slowly through it until you reach the ring fence, then immediately turn left or right, turning the horse toward one of the bunches of cattle and away from the ring fence. The half of the herd that you're now following is very likely to suddenly swing back toward the center of the ring, going around you, to rejoin the others at your back. If this happens, jump the horse out toward the heads of the back-circling cows and turn them away. This is easier said than done. You must "switch gears" in a hurry, going from the walk into a quick spurt at the gallop and then reining into the retreating cows. The green horse may be a trifle startled by this sudden demand for instant speed, but he will soon respond because he has developed some "cow" and wants to go to the cattle. His rein training now comes into play. He is physically prepared and his trailing work makes him responsive to the cattle's moves. But the rider must be equally quick—this is your first brush with really going after stock. Remember to first cue with the legs, the dwell operates here. Keep the seat secure, but let the upper body be flexible, even limp. You must go with the sudden impulsion of the horse; if not, you're going to be left behind. You can expect a sensation of your upper body being "whipped" by the swift, even jolting, motions of the horse. You will become accustomed to this in time and you will barely notice it. There are some mechanical aids that will help you, too. If you are serious about riding stock horses, you'll likely use a cutting-horse-type saddle, flat in the seat, low in front, with a slight undercut swell (as earlier described). Your stirrups will be narrow, one-inch models, either oxbows or flat tread, with your feet fully home for security, the tread against your heel.[3] Don't expect that in riding stock horses your leg position will always be fixed (as is appropriate in earlier forms of equitation); the

[3]This is the reason for the high, underslung heels of the traditional western boot. Low-heeled, "walking-heel" boots are now popular, but for stock-horse riding, most experienced hands prefer the traditional high heel, myself included.

157

Mike Mowery, a rising star in cutting and son of Bill Mowery (a veteran of the cutting-horse fraternity), working a cow. Mike's position is deep and in the middle of the horse, legs firmly used against the horse's barrel. He has attained an excellent balance.

One of the stars of the cutting-horse ring, Don Dodge of Scottsdale, Arizona. Notice the supple relaxation of the rider's position. The seat is deep, but not stiff. The security of Don's position is revealed by the lack of tension in his hand and forearm.
Credit: Louise L. Serpa

sequences of quick moves by the horse makes this virtually impossible, in the first place, and, second, you need to move your legs as, in order to balance in the stirrups, the legs must often swing. A short-turning stock horse or cutting horse may almost put the tread of one stirrup on the ground. And there is no crime in using the saddlehorn for grip. All cutting-horse riders operate with the free hand on the horn and stock-horse riders will grab the horn intermittently.

If you succeed in turning back that part of the herd, rein up. Let the cattle come back together. Separating the herd is a preamble, so to speak, to being able to work a single cow out of the herd. That is your next assignment.

FACE TO FACE WITH A COW

Enter the herd again. but this time not exactly at dead center. How to move into a herd with the object of cutting out a single animal is a much discussed subject among stock-horse and cutting-horse men, and it is surprisingly complex, due to all sorts of considerations. In competitive cutting, it is an important tactical decision. For our purposes, we simply want to initially break the herd into uneven parts so that we can select our "target" animal from the smaller group, at least in the beginning. As you turn with the bunch you've decided to follow, put the horse's head immediately on the single animal you're after and follow. As you move after this cow, the others accompanying it— say three or four—will peel off away from it, perhaps in both directions. Your target cow may proceed for a short distance, but it will be quickly aware of its lonely position. It will turn away to rejoin the herd. Let's assume that you're working to the left, counterclockwise of the ring, with the ring fence on your right. What you want to do is to bring the cow into the fence and then turn it left, so that it will follow the fence line away from the herd at your back. If the cow has drifted well toward the center of the ring, it may duck left; if it is fairly near the fence, it will likely duck right into the fence. In most cases, a cow will prefer to go against the fence and that is a helpful inclination. The best place to be in this situation is slightly to the left of the cow's rump as it begins its turn. That will give you a jump on it if it ducks left, and

Facing the cow. It is necessary to encourage the inexperienced horse to be both alert and calm. The horse shown here is a three-year-old Quarter Horse of Doc Bars breeding.

if it chooses to go right, toward the fence, you can aid that turn by moving alongside it, reining toward its head.

If the cow ducks right, your problem is to take it to the fence, but prevent it from doubling back along the fence to the right. This means that you must stay *very* close to the cow, coming onto its right side, "aiming" your horse at its head. There is a pretty good general rule in stock-horse work: go for the head. This often means, in practice, going at speed for the fence—and that's an unsettling experience at first. This is where your hours of work at "doubling" pay off. In the hypothetical example we're using, you must come into the fence on the right side of the cow, moving toward its head, "doubling back" now to the left, turning the cow sharply and moving it parallel to the fence. This is the classic stock-horse maneuver. It is not easy, particularly the first few tries. If the fence is wire, you may hear your chaps brush against the mesh as you double back.

The success of this maneuver calls for a level of horsemanship that's subliminal. You don't have time to calculate; the horse must be, in truth, an extension of your own thought and will. It is a matter of timing. If you over-ride the cow, it will turn left, all right, but will instantly duck behind you rather than follow the fence line. If you're late, if you don't go deep into the ring fence, the cow will duck around you to the right.

It would be handy if this tactic could be done in slow motion so you could gain confidence at a relatively slow pace—and it does make sense to try to use slower cattle if you can. But this is a case where you have to jump in and get your feet wet. Be satisfied, at first, if you can cut out a single cow and take it to the fence. That is an accomplishment and one that cannot be gained, either, without a few failures, perhaps numerous failures.

OTHER STOCK-HORSE MANEUVERS

In competition, in reined-cow-horse events, stock horses are required to work a single cow down a fence line, work it back along the same fence line, bring it to the center of the ring, and hold it there, circling in both directions around it. This is what you must be able to do if you decide to enter reined-cow-horse competition. Additionally, in most competitions, reined cow horses are asked to run a standard, "dry" reining pattern and the score is an aggregate between what the horse earns on this pattern and on the cattle work just described.

Don't try to master all these moves at once. As a matter of fact, stock horses tend to get sour if given too much "formalized" cattle work. Don't practice the competitive sequence as much as just working cattle, trailing, entering the herd, cutting out individual animals and small bunches. This work calls into play all the skills of the reining horse: short turns, spins, stops, acceleration of gait, *plus* an increasing initiative and cow sense on the part of the horse, to the point, even, where the horse can act independently. The cutting horse, naturally, operates with an almost total initiative; the reined cow horse, too, employs a great deal of independent initiative, although the conditions under which the cow horse works call for more actual reining on the part of the rider. A good cow horse senses a cow's moves more quickly than the rider in most cases, I believe.

It is necessary, though, that you now learn to work a cow up and down a fence line as well as just getting the animal there. There are times when this is startlingly simple. Once in a while a cow will obediently trot down the arena side, once turned; you can simply double back ahead of it at the other end and it will

161

Taking the cow down the fence. The rider works just off the cow's haunches, watching the "target" carefully. He is prepared to cue with the hands and legs, but allows the horse some initiative.

Taking the cow off the fence. The rider has turned the cow quickly, the horse pressing its flank. This is a maneuver in which the horse must stay close. Here, the young horse is quite eager to stick with his cow.

compliantly turn and jog back down the side again. That's serendipity. More often, though, the cow is far less cooperative.

The key to a smooth run down the fence line is to keep the cow moving evenly, to crowd it enough so that it doesn't get too much of a chance to think about ducking back. A dangerous moment is when the cow is first turned away into the fence. The act of going into the fence and turning the cow along it frequently slows up the horse and rider to the degree that the rider is not immediately on the cow, pushing it. There is an instant of deliberation and in that split second the initiative is lost; the cow ducks away and is temporarily lost. The doubling figure (for that is what it really is) that brings the cow to the fence, blocks it, turns it, and moves it up the side of the arena must be one motion. Too many times the horse, head into the fence, is turned and then checked, allowing the cow to escape. To jump out after the cow, upon completion of the doubling figure, should be immediate but also controlled, a natural extension of the turn. If it is not controlled, there is a risk that the horse can speed past a cow that stops, ducks low into the fence, and dodges in the other direction. The horse must jump out, of course, on the side of the cow away from the fence, keeping the cow between the horse and the arena side.

Be careful to watch the cow as it moves forward. With a little experience, you can gauge whether the cow is accelerating to make a nice parallel run along the fence or is slowing down, likely preparing to stop and duck. By all means keep the cow moving, even crowding it enough to cause it to increase speed, your horse, preferably, just off the cow's haunches. Should the cow stop and duck, spin away from it and pursue, going for its head so that a quick doubling into the fence will turn it back. If the cow really gets ahead of you and then turns well into the arena, let it have room to move, to straighten itself up, moving your horse deeper toward the arena center and then force the cow to the fence and double it back. If it turns shorter, ahead of you, you may be able to come up and, facing it, cause it to turn away and go in the opposite direction. But this is a dangerous tactic, because with loads of room the cow can run past you on either side.

Turning the cow back at the opposite end of the arena is not the most difficult of your problems because the cow wants to turn back anyway. But you don't want a premature duck-out, and you do want to turn the cow on the fence and not in the arena corner

163

or toward the center of the ring. As you approach the end of the long side of the arena, move your horse away from the cow's rump by just a few feet so that you are in better position to go to its head. Do this fairly gradually as you move along the fence, as you don't want the cow to get the idea that it can double back between you and the fence. Then jump out in a hurry, go to the head, and double the cow back, coming right after it, stationing yourself just off its haunches.

The cow will likely increase speed of its own accord. He *may* be headed in the direction he wants to go, but he just might decide to save a little ground by cutting across the ring.[4] Stick close to the cow, because turning it at the end of the arena may be a tough job. You may be in a "horse race" down the arena side, and you must be prepared to cut into the fence ahead of the cow in order to turn it. You'll probably have to "turn it on."

The doubling-back of the cow can be done in the usual way, except that at the conclusion of this turn you should be *between* the cow and the fence, moving it away from the fence line. This the cow is likely to resist, trying to get around you, or, pushed toward the center of the arena, it may make a mad dash for the pens, particularly if you are close to one of the pens well filled with other cattle. You must be prepared for either move as you come off the fence.

The center of the arena is the last place the cow wants to go. It's easier to get it there if you can succeed in keeping it moving once you have turned it from the fence. Hurry it on and don't let it really stop in front of you when you reach the center if you can avoid it; rather, circle at once so that your movement will cause the cow to turn and face you. Don't dawdle on the circle; you want to get it over with while you've got the cow's attention, so to speak. Reverse direction and circle again, keeping an eye trained on the cow. It'll mill around some and might even try to make a run for it. For this reason, keep the circles reasonably small—not so small as to alarm the cow but small enough to pressure it all the time, confusing it momentarily.

[4] Stock-horse competition is affected by the "luck of the draw" in this way: cattle are held in pens at one end of the arena and released one by one for use. After use, they are corralled at the opposite end in another pen. If you draw a cow early in the competition, then it is likely to want to return to the first pen where most of its companions are. If you draw later, your cow is apt to want to get to the other pen where by now most of the rest of the cattle are held. Keep this in mind.

Age is no factor. This is Dan Marshall, age twelve, winning the 1977 All American Amateur Cutting Horse Tournament at St. Louis.

Credit: Barry Dierkes

I repeat: don't try to reproduce this sequence of moves that are the core of public competition every time you work your horse. Mostly let the horse work "free," that is move and sort cattle more spontaneously.

TEAM PENNING

"Team penning" is an actual event in reined-cow-horse competitions, and perhaps you and some friends may want to try it. I introduce it here not primarily as a competitive event, but as a learning situation. Also, novice cutting-horse riders often start getting experience by riding "turn back" during cutting sessions. It's excellent experience, but it ought to be kept in mind that "turn-back" men are an important part of cutting and to perform the job calls for a considerable amount of experience to begin with. Team penning, I think, is the ideal training ground for stock-horse riders.

The "rules" are simple. At one end of a large arena is a small herd, some of the animals bearing a distinctive mark, like a temporary white cross. At the opposite end of the arena is a small catch pen. The aim of the game is for a team of three riders to cut

165

out those marked cows and deposit them in the pen. This undertaking provides a wide variety of possible situations; the tactics involved may be highly varied, too. In practice use, it is not necessary, of course, to have a team of three; you can use two or four or even more riders and you needn't be concerned with the time element, either. As a matter of fact, in the practice situation, it is probably better if you don't try to hurry, but let the cattle more or less determine how quick you must move. Team penning under these practice conditions quite closely approximates the sort of duty done by stock horses on working ranches. Indeed, if you ever have the opportunity to work cattle under range conditions, jump at the chance because the experience for your horse is excellent. Cattle on ranches are worked slowly for the obvious reason that you don't want to run off weight, and this consideration makes actual ranch work a splendid training ground for the young horse. Many top cutting-horse trainers prefer to have their young horses work cattle for a time under actual ranch conditions. It is my opinion that reining horses (who in the show ring will never actually confront a live cow) need a certain amount of cattle work to offset the monotony of just running dry patterns; it gives them a new lease on life, encourages their initiative.

Horsemanship on the Working Stock Horse

So far we have been discussing the tactics of riding the stock horse—how to use the horse with cattle. There is, in a sense, little that is actually new to you in the techniques of horsemanship, except two elements: (1) the speed and quickness of maneuver are intensified; (2) part of the time the rider may be reacting to the initiative of the horse, rather than wholly directing his actions. This second element is not unique to stock horses. Take, for example, the problem of riding the jumping horse over a fence. Regardless of the disputed theory involved, the horse, when jumping, actually determines the precise instant of its takeoff. The rider must therefore follow the horse, attempting to keep his own weight in close relationship to the horse's center of gravity. This is a matter, again, of a highly trained "conditioned response." But it is also an example of the ability to "sit still," because once the horse begins his jumping movement, elevates

166

his forehand to clear the obstacle, the rider's weight is a sheer handicap and the rider wants to disturb the horse's balance as little as possible. These considerations—quickness of response, being close to the center of gravity, and "sitting still"—apply, in general, to riding the stock horse as well.

The quickness of reaction time is largely a matter of practice, provided the basic position of the rider is sound to begin with. It entails a subconscious knowledge of what the horse is doing under you. It will come in time if you remain very aware of the need to analyze the consistency of your position. As I have said before, your ability to use the rein with finesse depends on the balance you get from your "seat." This subliminal reaction is the paramount skill of the cutting-horse rider.

You must stay close to the center of gravity. In practical terms, on a stock horse, this means not coming away, leaning away, from the thrust of the horse. It is easy to get whiplashed, which causes the upper body, even the lower torso, to be jerked to the rear. You are not only behind then, but you're handicapping the horse by allowing your weight momentarily but crucially to be displaced from its center of gravity. The upper body, however, cannot be stiff, as I've said earlier, not even as rigid as would be proper for ordinary equitation; it must move with the horse, even at times being behind the line of the legs, but it should never be allowed to slant severely backward. And the lower body—the hip region— should remain solidly and consistently in the saddle with the legs for support. Weight distribution in the stirrups, already discussed, varies when riding reining patterns or working a stock horse, balance depending upon quick movements of weight into the stirrup on the turning side.

It is desirable to sit still on a stock horse, but this is, after all, only a figure of speech. Following the rapid motions of the horse obviously means that the body is not immobile like a statue. It does imply, more literally, though, three things: (1) basic balance is always preserved; (2) the lower body does not move horizontally back and forth in the saddle—you don't want to be slipping back and forth from swells to cantle; (3) all *unnecessary* movement of the body is eliminated. The capacity of the horse to perform the feats of agility demanded of the stock horse is affected by the parallel ability of the rider to keep his body near the horse's center of gravity; the horse cannot move well hauling a loose, flapping, lurching burden. The actual weight of the rider is not in itself much of a factor; a two-hundred-pound-plus rider is not at a marked disadvantage. But the consistency with which that weight is kept against the horse's spinal column is a factor. Some stock-horse riders look like acrobats on the backs of their horses; some, on the other hand, seem to settle down into the middle of their horses and stay there. The latter style is to be much preferred.

It is hard to talk in precise terms about "timing," but nonetheless it is an attribute vital to riding stock horses well. By "timing" I mean the ability to "make moves" at the right time, usually a matter of a split second. Timing demands not only instantaneous decision-making but also an equally rapid transmission of cues. The less strenuous these cues need to be, the more quickly they can be applied and the quicker the reaction. There is a temptation in the heat of work to over-ride horses, that is, to become crude in applying leg and hand cues. This coarseness of aids actually interferes with timing, and it usually is the result of being caught a little flat-footed by the cow, itself a failure of timing. The cow horse should be ridden with dash, aggressively, going "all out," but this shouldn't mean that you over-ride the horse by thrashing your legs or jerking the reins. There is a rule that applies universally to riding all well-schooled horses whether they are stock horses, hunters, polo ponies, or pleasure horses: *let the horse work.* Don't interfere, in other words, with the capacity of the trained horse to do what he knows how to do. It's a partnership—which makes working horses a sport in a class by itself.

What's Ahead?

It's not too hard to see what's ahead. The whole lifelong process of *horsemastership* opens up, now channeled to some extent into those specialties that by now you have developed an enthusiasm to try. In this chapter, I have stressed riding the stock horse as a way of introducing this transition from "rider" to "horseman." But there are few things as fascinating or challenging as learning the high art of cutting (considerable groundwork for which has been laid in this book). Roping can become a rewarding and healthy addiction. Riding a fine pleasure horse is one of life's higher-ranked pleasures. Trail riding of all kinds is a world apart, and that is why, perhaps, it's so appealing. But even beyond western horsemanship, the gratification provided by horses is vast: foxhunting is certainly a noble sport; show jumping is a unique and exhilarating art; dressage is an engrossing blend of physical skill, art, and intellect. Driving horses is a thoroughly enjoyable pastime—and any well-grounded horseman of any type should be familiar with how to drive a horse. There are more experiences to be had than a lifetime can encompass.

Perhaps that's the eternal fascination of horsemastership: one person can never "master" it all. The learning we started in this book is just a beginning, in truth. The digestion of knowledge and skill goes on, especially in terms of developing the capacity to train as well as to ride. It is open-ended. Every horse you'll ever sit on will teach you something, however slight, that you didn't know before. Of course, you've got to remain susceptible to the process. And even the passing of years will not blunt that continuing quest any more than it will dull your satisfactions and even skills. Some activities are limited by age. Not horsemanship. What you may lose later in quickness of physical reaction will be compensated for by experience and craft. There is no reason why you can't work a stock horse as well at seventy as at thirty. And there are few equestrian activities (except, perhaps, throwing a three-hundred-pound calf) that women can't compete in on exactly equal terms.

One question I've been asked a thousand times or more: "Aren't horses a very expensive hobby?" I've developed a stock answer: "Yes, they are if they are only a secondary, less than vital interest. But, if they're not, if they're a central part of your life, especially a family's life, then they're cheap at the price." With today's rising feed costs, I'd be inclined to add to that that it makes sense to keep a "good" horse because a poor one costs just as much to feed, granted that the designation "good" may be a personal judgment. The point I'm trying to make is that keeping a horse is no more costly than most popular hobbies (except collecting beer cans or bird-watching, maybe), but you ought to get as much fun out of it as possible and that means having a horse that can do something. The trouble is that most people approach buying their first horse as if they're acquiring a family dog or even

169

getting married. If you're smart, you'll understand that your first horse ought to be a "learning" horse and not the animal of your ultimate dreams, and that there will come a time when you've gotten all that the horse has to give, in terms of experience, and you'll need a more challenging, more competitive animal. As you grow in skill, you will have different requirements. Most people, I've discovered, tend to be too ambitious in selecting a first horse; they are tempted to buy a horse too young, too green, too "fancy." They are often aided and abetted in this by horse dealers, incidentally, but that's another yarn. A typical myth— what I call the "puppy syndrome"—rests upon believing in the feasibility of an inexperienced child getting along with a half-broke colt, growing up together, as it were. This is the stuff of TV dramas, but it doesn't work in real life—at least not often enough to make any sense.

For your first horse, just in passing, you might consider four possible sources (assuming you don't have the help of a responsible professional): (1) a privately owned horse that has served someone else as a "transitional" horse, the owner having "graduated" to a more competitive animal. It's helpful to know the party involved, though. (2) A not-too-green horse that wasn't quite sharp enough for the show ring, though basically sound in disposition, manners, and ability, a horse that was not quite "showy" enough to be a ribbon-winner. (3) A "school horse" from a really top-quality riding school. Be careful here. You don't want a "dude" or a livery horse, but a horse that has been carefully used for serious instruction. (4) A well-seasoned working ranch horse might be attractive, but, of course, he'd have to be evaluated as an individual. Some ranch horses are pretty common, but some other ranch animals are breedy and right-headed.

A few more quick tips on making that fateful investment: regardless of whom you buy the horse from, have a vet check it for health and soundness. The seller might not be trying to hide anything, but he might not have discovered some serious impairment. Don't expect to find some bargain-basement wonder. You can hear tales about horses coming out of "killer pens" that went on to become champions, and I've owned a "Cinderella" horse or two in my time (but out of, heaven knows, how many?). You don't need to spend a bundle on a serviceable horse for your first experience at ownership, but you need to pay a fair market value

An authentic breed of the American West—the Quarter Horse. This fine stallion is AQHA Champion Skip's Alibi, owned by Pretty Penny Ranch of Scottsdale, Arizona. This horse combines excellence at both halter and steer roping. Credit: Darol Dickinson Photo

Another native American—the Appaloosa. Originally the war and hunting horse of the Nez Perce Indians, the Appaloosa developed into a tough stock horse. This excellent stallion is Dial Bright Too, a champion both at halter and in racing.

for something that's useful. Prices of horses range from what they're worth by the pound to almost any astronomical figure you can think of. For a good "learning" horse, you pay for what abilities he has that you think you want. A good stock horse that you can learn that game on will have a price tag that's higher because of the increased training that's gone into him, along with some innate ability, too. Prospective competitive reined cow horses, cutting horses, and rope horses are expensive items. Ring-quality pleasure horses, show-type trail horses, and reining horses are, of course, valuable merchandise for the silverware they can collect for you. I don't think there are really any critical differences between mares and geldings—although registered mares can sometimes be taken as a tax deduction. Stallions belong in a special category.

This is hardly an exhaustive treatise on horse-buying, and I mention the subject only to suggest some practical considerations concerning your first horse purchase if you're faced with it. All horses represent compromises; the perfect horse has not yet been foaled or trained. Enjoy your horse for what he is. Appreciate his merits; be realistic about his deficiencies.

And Finally—the Transition to Training

Horse training is a high art, and surprisingly few people become real masters of it. This is because the trainer must be able to combine within himself a demanding combination of theoretical knowledge, experience, personal temperament, and discipline. Additionally, every horse is different and that calls for imagination and flexibility. These comments about training are valid enough in the context of comprehensive professional-level training, but they ought not to obscure the fact that riding and training are inseparable functions and at a certain level of skill—the skill you've gained by the conclusion of this book—the act of riding begins to significantly affect the behavior of the horse. Isn't that training? Put another way, when you ride your horse he is no longer a "learning device"; you want to improve, however modestly, the excellence of his performance when you ride him. That means, in turn, that your skill as a rider is finally dedicated to your function as trainer.

172

You cannot train a car. The only thing that affects the behavior of a car is its mechanical condition. This being consistent, your car will behave the same every time you drive it. Your horse, on the other hand, may be *different* every time you ride it. This difference may be very slight (and may in part be the result of its physical nature and even its day-to-day moods), but the real source of the difference in its behavior is *you*. Every time you ride it, the horse will either improve or deteriorate in quality, if ever so slightly. That's a startling thought, don't you agree? A superbly trained ten-thousand-dollar animal can quickly become a useless rogue worth a fraction of its purchase price in the hands of an ignorant, clumsy owner-rider. Training, therefore, is something you can't avoid.

But you don't want to avoid it, because training is, as you can imagine, the ultimate goal and gratification of horsemanship. Learning to train is like learning to ride: it cannot be done overnight—even if you possess the theory involved. Sometimes the urge to train prompts people to undertake more than they're ready for. It's hardly good sense to encourage a teenage beginner to buy an unbroke two-year-old and try to develop it. Don't suppose you can go out and buy a green colt and turn it into a champion cutting horse. Have reasonable expectations—like gradually improving the capabilities of the horse you've got by patient repetition. Seventy-five percent of training is slow, routine repetition that does not necessarily call for unusual gifts of aptitude or decades of experience. The other twenty-five percent does. But that doesn't mean you can't operate, from the start, within the sphere of the less adroit aspects of training.[5] You may well master, in time, that more elusive twenty-five percent anyway. Become, therefore, training-oriented. Don't just "ride"—*train*. If you can say that the horse you've just gotten down off of is just a little better for your having ridden it, then you're a horseman.

---

[5] In the past I have experimented very successfully with what could be called "cooperative training" with amateur horse owners. Under my supervision, they would do the bulk of the training, reserving for me the remainder. I don't think this is an ideal way to develop a top performance horse, but it is an approach that satisfactorily produces useful, pleasant horses and, more importantly, it is the source of great satisfaction and pleasure for the owners, providing a dimension of successful horsemastership previously not experienced by them.

173

Selected Bibliography on General Horse Care

Davidson, Joseph B., D.V.M. *Horseman's Veterinary Adviser.* New York: Arco Publishing Company, 1977.

Ensnimger, M.E. *Horses and Tack.* Boston: Houghton Mifflin and Company, 1977.

Evans; Borton; Hintz; and Van Vleck (eds.). *The Horse.* San Francisco: W.H. Freeman and Company, 1977.

Jacobson, Patricia, and Hayes, Marcia. *A Horse Around the House.* New York: Crown Publishing Company, 1972.

Laune, Paul. *America's Quarter Horses.* New York: Doubleday and Company, 1973.

Marlin, Herb, and Savitt, Sam. *How to Take Care of Your Horse Until the Vet Comes.* New York: Dodd Mead and Company, 1975.

Nariaux, James, L., D.V.M. *Horses in Health and Disease.* New York: Arco Publishing Company, 1976.

Posey, Jeanne K. *The Horse Keeper's Handbook.* New York: Winchester Press, 1974.

Price, Steven. *The Whole Horse Catalog.* New York: Simon and Schuster, 1978.

Sevelius, Fritz; Pettersson, Harry; and Olsson, Lennart. *Healthy Horse Handbook: The Owner's Illustrated Guide.* New York: David McKay Company, Inc., 1978.

Stoneridge, N.A. *A Horse of Your Own.* New York: Doubleday and Company, 1968.

Appendix

American Quarter Horse Association Specifications for the Stock and Hunt Seats*

STOCK SEAT

566. *Hands:* Both hands and arms shall be held in a relaxed easy manner with the upper arms to be in a straight line with the body, the one holding the reins bent at the elbow. Free hand will be partially closed and held near the belt with the elbow bent causing the hand to be near but not against the body in front of that side; however, when using the romal the rider's off hand shall be around the romal with at least 16 inches of slack. Some movement of the arm is permissible, but excessive pumping will be penalized. Hands to be around reins. One finger between the reins is permitted when using split reins, but not with romal. Reins are to be carried

---

*These specifications are reprinted from the *Official Handbook of the American Quarter Horse Association*, Twenty-fifth edition, January 1, 1977.
NOTE: These descriptions are provided for the reader's information. The author is not wholly in sympathy with all aspects of these specifications.

176

immediately above or slightly in front of the saddle horn. Only one hand is to be used for reining and hand shall not be changed. Reins should be carried so as to have light contact with the horse's mouth and at no time shall reins be carried more than a slight hand movement from the horse's mouth.

567. *Basic Position:* Rider should sit in saddle with legs hanging straight and slightly forward to stirrups. The stirrup should be just short enough to allow heels to be lower than toes. Body should always appear comfortable, relaxed and flexible. Feet may be placed home in the stirrups with boot heel touching the stirrup or may be placed less deep in the stirrup. Riding with toes only in the stirrup will be penalized.

568. *Position in Motion:* Rider should sit to trot and not post. At the lope he should be close to the saddle. All movements of the horse should be governed by the use of imperceptible aids. Exaggerated shifting of the rider's weight is not desirable. Moving of the lower legs of riders who are short shall not be penalized.

HUNT SEAT

579. *Hands:* Hands should be over and in front of the horse's withers, knuckles thirty degrees inside the vertical, hands slightly apart and making a straight line from the horse's mouth to rider's elbow. Method of holding reins is optional and bight of reins may fall on either side. However, all reins must be picked up at the same time.

580. *Basic Position:* The eyes should be up and shoulders back. Toes should be at an angle best suited to rider's conformation; ankles flexed in, heels down, calf of leg in contact with horse and slightly behind girth. Iron may be either on toe, ball of foot or "home."

581. *Position in Motion:* At the walk and slow trot, body should be vertical; posting trot, inclined forward; canter, halfway between the posting trot and the walk; galloping and jumping, same inclination as posting trot.

**Sample Reining
Class Patterns,
American Quarter
Horse Association**

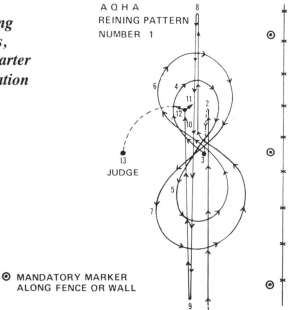

AQHA
REINING PATTERN
NUMBER 1

JUDGE

⊙ MANDATORY MARKER
ALONG FENCE OR WALL

The arena or plot should be approximately 50 × 150 feet in size. The judge shall indicate with markers on arena fence or wall the length of the pattern, markers within the area of the pattern will not be used.

Ride pattern as follows:

    1. to 2. Run with speed past center marker.

    2. Stop and back up to center of pattern.

    3. Settle horse for approximately 10 sec. Start lope to the right. Figure 8 should be made inside the end markers.

    4. & 5. Ride small Figure 8 at a slow lope.

    6. & 7. Ride a larger Figure 8 at a faster lope.

    8. Left roll back over hocks (should be made past far end marker.)

    9. Right roll back over hocks (should be made past near end marker.)

    10. Stop, (should be made past center marker) let horse settle, and in approximate area of stop, do the pivots.

    11. Pivot, right or left, no more than 90 degrees.

    12. Pivot opposite direction, no more than 180 degrees.

    13. Walk to judge and stop for inspection until dismised.

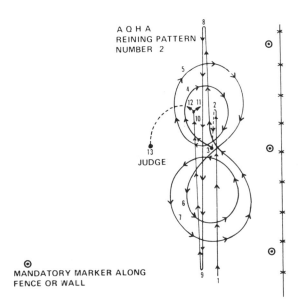

AQHA
REINING PATTERN
NUMBER 2

JUDGE

MANDATORY MARKER ALONG
FENCE OR WALL

The arena or plot should be approximately 50 × 150 feet in size. The judge shall indicate with markers on arena fence or wall the length of the pattern. Markers within the area of the pattern will not be used.

Ride pattern as follows:

1. to 2. Run with speed, past center marker.

2. Stop and back up to center of pattern.

3. Settle horse for approximately 10 sec. Start lope. Circles should be made inside the end markers.

4. & 5. Ride two circles to the right, first circle small, should be slow, and second circle larger and faster.

6. & 7. Ride two circles to the left, first circle small and slow, and second circle larger and faster.

8. Left roll back over hocks (should be made past far end marker).

9. Right roll back over hocks (should be made past near end marker).

10. Stop (should be made past center marker). Let horse settle, then in approximate area of stop, do the pivots.

11. Pivot right or left no more than 90 degrees.

12. Pivot opposite direction, no more than 180 degrees.

13. Walk to judge and stop for inspection until dismissed.

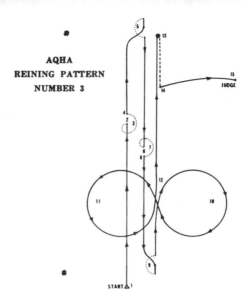

**AQHA
REINING PATTERN
NUMBER 3**

The arena or plot should be approximately 50 × 150 feet in size.
The judge shall indicate with markers on arena fence or wall the
length of the pattern, but kegs or other markers within the area of
the pattern will not be used.

Ride pattern as follows:

1. to 2. Run at full speed (should be at least 20 feet from any
fence or wall).

2. Stop.

3. Do a 360 degree spin.

4. Hesitate.

5. Proceed to the area beyond the point indicated by the marker
on the arena wall or fence and do a left roll back over the hocks.

6. Stop.

7. Do a 360 degree spin.

8. Hesitate.

9. Proceed to the area beyond the pont indicated by the other
marker on the arena wall or fence and do a right roll back over the
hocks.

10. & 11. Ride a figure 8, beginning to the right.

12. to 13. Run at full speed.

13. Stop

13. to 14. Back.

14. to 15. Walk to judge and stop for inspection until dismissed.

Index